QUEBEC 70

A DOCUMENTARY NARRATIVE / JOHN SAYWELL

UNIVERSITY OF TORONTO PRESS

Toronto and Buffalo
Printed in Canada
Reprinted 1972
ISBN 0-8020-6134-6
Reprinted from CANADIAN ANNUAL REVIEW FOR 1970

Contents

Preface

"If, once again, one can go by the climate of terror, the climate of violence, which has been the real outcome of separatism in the last ten years, one can think that the city in which we would live in an independent Quebec would certainly not be a very pleasant one," observed Prime Minister Pierre Trudeau before the Liberal Federation of Quebec on October 19, 1969. Looking back over the year about to end, it had been one of violence and terror, bombs and murder. All evidence pointed to the escalation of radicalism and nationalism, whether distinct or joined, in the province of Quebec. Only a few Canadians, however, took seriously the evidence that radical nationalists had adopted a strategy for revolution initially designed for banana republics and the Third World. Even those – in the press and public – who could read the signs seemed to dismiss them as idle rhetoric rather than impending reality. The fall of 1970 was to shatter all illusions as, in the language of the word merchants, the country "came of age" or "lost its innocence." It was unlikely that in his looking-glass even the Prime Minister foresaw the horror of October 1970.

The two kidnappings and the murder of Pierre Laporte were the biggest domestic news stories in Canada's history. For three months the media relentlessly pursued its story, doing little to enlighten Canadians on the tragic events but serving as the desired publicist for the Front de libération du Québec. For three months – and undoubtedly for years after 1970 – every journalist, every politician, every armchair strategist and instant historian, had his own interpretation and his own solution, both of which were commonly in line with his politics and ideology. Meanwhile, the country lived through a chapter of its history that was at once bizarre and tragic, unbelievable and terrifying. For three months Canadians knew literally only what the FLQ told them. Their communiqués were about the only hard news the public had, and it is their communiqués and official government statements that form much of the documentary narrative that follows. No useful purpose would seem to be served here by another account of the October crisis where fact and rumour, interpretation and polemics, were indistinguishable as they were in much of the reporting and in many of the instant books that followed hard on the heels of the crisis. This is an attempt to look at Quebec 70 as it happened, as the public and the governments experienced it, without the benefit of hindsight or the dangers of speculation.

Susan Merry and Michael Behiels helped with the research, and Pierre Pascau of CKLM, Montreal, was very helpful. All major documents and statements were translated by Edrica Baheux.

JOHN SAYWELL

Separatism or Federalism

APRIL 29

THE TRAGEDY of October seemed even more ironic because April 29 had brought unrestrained optimism to English Canada, for as the Toronto *Globe and Mail* expressed it: "the Province of Quebec is alive and well in Canada." Seldom, if ever, had a provincial election been so carefully watched; seldom, if ever, had a provincial election such national implications. And never had the results been as overwhelmingly approved outside a province as was Robert Bourassa's Liberal victory in the province of Quebec. Yet within six months the Canadian army had to be called in at the request of the young premier to prevent uncontrollable civil disorder, and some Québécois speculated on the collapse of the new government.

Amis de Robert Bourassa

By the beginning of 1970 the campaign for the succession to Jean Lesage as leader of the Liberal party of Quebec was nearing its end, with a convention scheduled for Quebec City on January 16–17. The style and strategy of the three contenders were strikingly different, their only common feature being a commitment to a resolution of Quebec's problems within a federal system. Pierre Laporte, the forty-eight-year-old veteran of a journalists' crusade against Maurice Duplessis and a member of the Lesage administration, counted on his popularity in the National Assembly. Claude Wagner, the forty-four-year-old law and order man of the Lesage régime, banked heavily on his undoubted popularity among a people tired of vandalism and crime, terror and violence. While both men emphasized the need for economic development, the thrust of Mr Wagner's appeal was that "the key to economic progress is political stability and social peace, respect of the law and individual liberties," while Mr Laporte called for a "competent society with a soul," a "society of participation" which would make "authority more efficient and more humane."

From the outset, however, it was hardly a contest, as both veterans were combatting a superior image and strategy. The image of Robert Bourassa – youth (thirty-six), education (law at Montreal, politics and economics at Oxford, and public finance at Harvard), cool and clipped manner, wealth (the husband of a Simard heiress), and experience (secretary of the Bélanger Commission and opposition financial critic) – seemed tailor-made for the position. Moreover, he was a protégé of Mr Lesage and, unlike Wagner and even Laporte, had since 1966 been the most loyal of party members; for although he harboured leadership ambitions he could afford to wait until Lesage's expected resignation in 1972.

A study submitted to Mr Lesage in May 1969 by Social Research Incorporated, an American firm, drew a portrait of the leader desired by the Quebec electorate. The electors desperately looked for "un chef," concluded SRI, a man who oozed confidence and knew where he was going, who was strong yet conciliatory, and who could bridge the generation gap – a leader who was "a good representative of the Quebec people, the kind of man who could be strong enough to deal with Ottawa, the titans of finance, and most aspects of a highly sophisticated urbanized world." It was almost the scenario for "Enter Bourassa," and it may have been convincing proof to Lesage that he should step down and give his encouragement, if not his open support, to Bourassa.

According to Gilles Racine (*La Presse*, September 14–19), within hours of Mr Lesage's resignation, Paul Desrochers, a Lesage aide and confidant, offered his support to Bourassa and became a key figure in the making of a leader and a prime minister. From Racine's account it would seem to have been Desrochers who outlined the strategy to be followed. Desrochers had studied at Columbia and in 1968 had spent six weeks among the Kennedy, Nixon, and Rockefeller teams. Having joined Bourassa, he immediately transferred the Draft Kennedy model into the "Friends of Robert Bourassa." Using a list of seventy-seven thousand members of the Parti libéral du Québec, drawn up a year earlier, Desrochers mailed seventy thousand cards on September 22, asking if the party members would support Bourassa for the leadership. By October 19, two days after Bourassa formally entered the race, sixteen thousand had answered "yes," providing the appearance of a popular movement as well as a magnificent base on which to build regional and constituency organizations. Over the next few months while Laporte and Wagner followed more traditional campaign strategies, the Bourassa team sewed up the election in the constituencies, and worked assiduously to secure student support. Well before the convention they virtually predicted the final result in the Quebec Coliseum.

It's auto show time

QUEBEC LIBERALS ARE LOOKING FOR A NEW MODEL IN LEADERS—
the BOURASSA
A SPORTS CAR DESIGNED FOR ECONOMIC PICK-UP WITH AN OPEN DOOR FOR FOREIGN INVESTMENT
the WAGNER
A SOLID MODEL WITH POLICE CAR LINES— GOES WELL ON COUNTRY ROADS —
LAW AND ORDER
the LAPORTE
STATION WAGON WITH ROOM FOR ALL BUT PARTY JUMPERS
EQUIPPED WITH EXPERIENCE SHOCK-ABSORBERS
ZAHN Collins

Gazette, Montreal, January 9, 1970

It was not all organization, however, as Mr Bourassa made the most of his image as the cool, efficient technocrat, who knew that the economy needed stimulus and knew how to produce it. He was also forthright in his attacks on separatism – billing himself as the leader who could defeat his old friend René Lévesque – and in his confidence that he had the capacity to stand up to the technocrats in Ottawa. Competence not confrontation would bring a better deal from Ottawa, he argued. English Canada strongly supported Mr Bourassa, and in Anglophone Quebec both the *Montreal Star*, which on January 12 pictured him as a "political realist" who would create a good businesslike administration, and the Montreal *Gazette* (January 16) urged his election. Although observers watched closely there was little sign of Ottawa's involvement. Yet while Labour Minister Bryce Mackasey openly supported Mr Wagner, his fellow Liberal from Verdun, most felt that the Prime Minister's Office probably was giving its quiet support to Bourassa.

As the campaign neared its end both Laporte and Wagner realized how effective the Bourassa strategy had been. On January 13 Mr Wagner charged that Mr Bourassa was spending a fortune, packing delegate meetings and offering summer jobs to students. On the eve of the convention the Laporte organization held a press conference, where Bourassa was accused of gross overspending and of being "the puppet of hidden financial interests." Eighteen pro-Laporte MNAs denounced the Bourassa campaign as a Montreal-based conspiracy, involving St James Street, the establishment, and the press: "We who are representing ridings where elections are won vote by vote and parish by parish against the Union Nationale machine; we who represent all the regions of Quebec; we who realize that the problems of Quebec are not as simple as economics or law and order, we believe that Pierre Laporte is the ideal candidate to lead us to victory." To the charge that he was rich Mr Bourassa sometimes replied that his wealth made him independent; and to charges that he was too young he replied that half the electorate was younger. Besides, wryly commented Alcide Courcy, the chief organizer for the party who had joined Bourassa on November 1, "old priests don't make the best bishops" – perhaps the only folksy comment in the Bourassa campaign.

As the delegates cast their ballots it was clear that organization had reaped its reward. Bourassa won easily on the first ballot with 843 votes to Wagner's 455 and Laporte's 288. Amid the cheers and the boos, Pierre Laporte rose to join the applause. But after a month of considering his future and apparently convinced that Bourassa would not end the influence of Jean Lesage in the party, Claude Wagner announced that he was resigning his seat and retiring from politics. The Wagner defection clearly expressed some of the tensions within the party – old and new, urban and rural – and did not augur well for the approaching election.

Towards April 29

Seldom, if ever, has a Quebec election been watched more closely by the English-Canadian media. Yet the general ignorance or indifference of much of the population may well offer its own comment on the likely success of the political and constitutional accommodation to nationalism and

Toronto Daily Star, April 23, 1970

biculturalism. For in a year that was to see the dramatic events of October, a Gallup Poll published on April 18 revealed that 39 per cent of Canadians could not say who they wanted to win in Quebec. Political allegiances die hard in the Maritimes and the west, where 18 and 16 per cent respectively opted for a Conservative victory although the Conservative party had not fought in a provincial election in Quebec since 1935. Only one thing was certain: virtually no one outside Quebec was a supporter of René Lévesque.

In retrospect, Jean-Jacques Bertrand's decision on March 12 to have a snap dissolution and an April 29 election seemed like a gross miscalculation. Yet if the Union nationale still suffered from ambiguities on policy and personal rivalries not yet stilled from its 1969 leadership convention, the party at least had its équipe, its patronage, and its finance. On the other hand, the Liberals had a new and untried leader and Mr Bourassa's scars of victory were still raw; the Ralliement créditiste, always a possible threat to the rural-based Union nationale, had a leadership convention before it; and René Lévesque's Péquistes were far from ready for an election. With a strike-promised summer, the decision seemed sound. And within a few days an election platform, promising everything but lower taxes, was ready for the electorate.

The Bourassa Liberals were far readier than Mr Bertrand imagined. The organization that had won the convention had retained its momentum. Within days of the announcement of the election the Liberals received the results of a small poll of thirty constituencies and five hundred voters, which gave the Liberals 18 per cent, the Parti québécois 14.3 per cent, the Union nationale 12.6, the Créditistes 9.3, and left 42.6 undecided. Not only did the Liberals accept the validity of the poll and conclude that Lévesque was their major enemy, but they also accepted the poll's insight into the issues that disturbed the electorate: unemployment, 47.8 per cent; education, 17.5 per cent; the economy, 10 per cent; high taxes, 9.6 per cent; industrialization, 9.3 per cent; the high cost of living, 6.3 per cent. Well behind these interrelated issues were questions of language, separatism, and provincial autonomy which concerned only 3, 1.5, and .5 per cent of the population respectively. QUEBEC TO WORK! became the slogan and "100,000 new jobs in 1971!" the promise; the means a Liberal team of competent administrators headed by the cool and confident technocrat running a Quebec that remained resolutely within "un fédéralisme rentable." As Mr Bourassa hammered home the Liberal theme, Liberal organizers built up a formidable organization and blanketed the province with carefully planned radio and television programmes and flying visits from Mr Bourassa. By February 16 Paul Desrochers predicted victory in 72 seats, and on the eve of the election Liberal organizers claimed to be certain of 62 and named a dozen others where the odds favoured the party.

René Lévesque's appeal was as direct in its essentials as Mr Bourassa's. Across from the large ads "Quebec: to work" was a picture of Mr

Lévesque urging the electorate to vote "YES." "We are – Québécois" read the lettering on the blackboard, while bold type declared:

THE TIME HAS COME TO SAY: YES
YES, to normal liberty in friendship with others.
YES, to normal security, and an end to prying.
YES, to normal responsibility, which is the only true driving force for progress at every level, beginning with the economy.
YES, quite simply to a normal life in a normal Quebec.
YES, on April 29, let's vote for Quebec.

Lévesque appealed to the young, the left, and the discontented, to those tired of the old parties and the wasted energy of decades of conflict with Ottawa. Although his programme was starkly nationalist, his tone was not shrill as he urged the Québécois not to believe that the economic price of independence was high and pleaded with them to withdraw their old fears and their subservient attitude towards English Canada and the local establishment. On the controversial language issue he promised both to make French the only official language and to respect the educational rights of the minority.

Just as Bourassa had selected the Péquistes as his prime target, so did Lévesque spend most of his time attacking the Liberals. He was concerned too that the Créditistes, under their new provincial leader Camil Samson, would pick up discontented votes in the rural areas from the flagging Union nationale which might otherwise have gone Parti québécois. By April 26 he was charging that the Créditistes were being manipulated by the Liberal machine – others suggested that the Liberals were not sorry to see the Créditistes in the field – and urged them to join the Parti québécois and help "clean house."

Mr Samson, meanwhile, was running a predictable campaign, appealing to rural discontent, applying conventional Social Credit solutions to the problems of poverty and unemployment, and arguing that the federal system was workable provided Quebec had control over credit and all matters within its jurisdiction, including direct taxation and social welfare.

As the three opposition parties – the provincial NDP was never a factor even in the eleven Montreal seats where it ran candidates – maintained a furious momentum, the Union nationale appeared to stagger and then collapse. The party began the election without a coherent platform, and remained throughout on the defensive. Prime Minister Bertrand's promise on April 5 that the UN would hold a referendum on independence by 1974 unless a new constitution had been drafted (apparently at the urging of Finance Minister Mario Beaulieu) seemed to be a futile attempt to find middle ground between Bourassa's federalism and Lévesque's independence. Without satisfying the more nationalistic members of the Union nationale it may even have forced UN members into the Liberal, PQ, or Créditiste camps. The UN position was further weakened when Marcel Masse, speaking to students at Ste Foy on April 22, declared that the only difference between the Union nationale and the Parti québécois was that of immediate independence or waiting on events until 1974. Reprimanded by Bertrand, Mr Masse then even suggested the possibility of a UN-PQ coalition if the government found itself in a minority.

Long before the election the Union nationale appeared to be "running scared." The promises became more generous – more unlikely of fulfilment too as Mr Beaulieu forecast a billion dollar deficit at an April 10 press conference – and the attack on Ottawa's miserliness more strident. A *La Presse* poll, published on April 18, revealed that the Union nationale had fallen to third place with only 13.4 per cent of the votes. A *Montreal Star* poll of a few constituencies, published on April 25, also showed the UN trailing the Liberals and the Péquistes, as did a Peter Regenstreif poll published in the *Toronto Star* (April 24) which gave the Liberals 32 per cent, the PQ 23, the UN 16, and the Créditistes 9. The polls enabled the Union nationale to charge that the press was against them, while Mr Bertrand gamely replied that he was out to win elections, not polls. But the polls and the opposition of most newspapers to the UN provided the opportunity to lash out in a last desperate attack on his enemies. On April 26, while Justice Minister Rémi Paul was asserting that while not all Péquistes were terrorists all terrorists were members of the Parti québécois and that Lévesque was the Castro of Quebec, Mr Bertrand was picturing the election as a giant plot of the financiers to destroy him. In a speech apparently only partly delivered because his audience sat on their hands, he linked the newspaper polls with the financial interests of Montreal and Toronto. The *Montreal Star* and the *Gazette* might be expected to support the Liberals but he took special pains to point out that *La Presse* was owned by the Power Corporation, and rang all the changes on the links between the Power Corporation and the Liberal party from Peter Nesbitt Thomson (first vice-chairman of the board) to Marc Lalonde and Mr Bourassa's brothers-in-law. "Don't we have the right to ask questions in the face of the tentacles we see that link all these men to the Liberal party, provincially and federally?" But in the last few days he seemed to move away from that bravado to urge traditional UN supporters not to be complacent and to ask for a law and order mandate to stamp out radicals and terrorists.

Lost in the constitution woods

Gazette, Montreal, April 24, 1970

The issues of French-English and federal-provincial relations could hardly be kept out of the campaign. Mr Bourassa did his best to minimize them, refusing to be drawn into constitutional discussions about "fédéralisme rentable" and arguing that while "French must be the working language of Quebec, we don't have to break up Canada to achieve that goal." But both Beaulieu and Lévesque kept hammering away at the old tax game, picturing a virtuous Quebec as the innocent victim of federal rape. Mr Beaulieu continually drew attention to the $200 million that Quebec claimed from taxes levied to finance medicare, and on April 23 published in *Le Devoir* a letter to Finance Minister Edgar Benson in which he wondered why justice was not done to Quebec when the wheat farmers collected $100 million, Nova Scotia $40 million, and recipients of foreign aid the $200 million recommended by Lester Pearson.

Throughout this attack both Mr Bourassa and the federal Liberals remained quiet. But on April 23 the Quebec wing of the Liberal party of Canada published it 250,000-circulation monthly bulletin, *Quoi de Neuf*. The bulletin provided a detailed breakdown of all figures and concluded that in 1968–69 Quebec gained $547 million. The bulletin added that the federal government employed more than ninety thousand Québécois, purchased $357 million worth of goods in Quebec, and would invest more than $400 million in Quebec during the fiscal year. The annual net gain, claimed *Quoi de Neuf*, was more than one billion dollars. The editors claimed to be reluctant to enter the controversy, but wrote that "For several years ... the federal government has refused to engage in this sterile discussion which seeks to measure the advantages of federalism in auditing terms. It is nonetheless true that these provincial politicians who try to make us believe that we are being toyed with by Ottawa, with the aid of figures which they carefully avoid explaining because they can't do it, have spread fears which must be dissipated." Questioned in Ottawa, Secretary of State Gérard Pelletier shrugged off the suggestion that this was federal intervention: "I think it has always been understood amongst us that when Confederation is threatened, we could not stand idly by ... We would reply with facts and figures and answers. That is what we have done" (*Ottawa Citizen*, April 24). Bertrand and Lévesque immediately hailed the document as proving their charges that Bourassa was a puppet of Ottawa. Mr Bourassa himself denounced the document as a "bulletin de propagande" which contained debatable figures and its publication as "badly timed, awkward, and without justification." Not for the first or last time, Prime Minister Trudeau was forced to undercut one of his Quebec ministers. On April 26 his office issued a press release stating that

Mr Bertrand's accusation of federal intervention was an "accusation without foundation." The bulletin was published by the party "without prior approval or censorship of the federal government in general and of its prime minister in particular as is normal in a truly democratic party." Ottawa had not intervened, the statement concluded, "and in spite of the provocation of certain provincial politicians, it does not intend to do so."

Although the Bourassa Liberals were aware of the danger that could come from Ottawa's intervention, there were many English Canadians who waited for the Trudeau team to swing into action. Alarmed by the apparent strength of Lévesque, the *Globe and Mail* wondered editorially on April 21 whether the time had not come for Mr Trudeau to enter the campaign:

> It is tradition to assume that Quebec resents any Ottawa intervention in its provincial elections, but this is not a provincial election like any other provincial election. The fate of the country could be riding upon it.
>
> Mr. Trudeau and his Quebec colleagues have a duty to present to their constituents the federal side of the issue and point out the folly of electing a party committed to breaking up the country.
>
> They have plenty of ammunition to use, for a separated Quebec would be an impoverished and unhappy place, and Mr. Lévesque, as La Presse has pointed out, has left all of the hard facts out of his pretty picture of sovereignty. Mr. Trudeau is also the only man with an emotional currency in Quebec to match that of Mr. Lévesque. He cannot leave the field to him until after April 29.

Some observers felt that position was shared by many MPs.

Within Quebec the English-Canadian minority worked valiantly to secure Mr Bourassa's victory. On April 3 the Montreal investment firm of Lafferty and Hardwood advised its clients to ship their securities and liquid assets outside the province until after the election. The Montreal dailies left no doubt of their position. And on April 26 the Royal Trust openly sent a shipload of securities out of the province in nine Brinks trucks. Whether these ploys led the timid to vote Liberal rather than PQ or UN could not be determined, but they certainly fanned the flames of separatist anger and undoubtedly did little to ease English-French relations within the province.

On the eve of the election the Montreal press attempted to provide its readers with an overview of the campaign. The *Gazette*, editorially committed to the Liberals, provided a comparative chart of the parties' platforms on key issues:

Jean-Jacques Bertrand NATIONAL UNION	Robert Bourassa LIBERAL
Constitution and independence	
The National Union is pledged to bring about a new Canadian constitution which would respect the fundamental rights of Quebec as the national home of French-speaking Canadians. The revision is stalled because of the rigid, intolerant and arrogant attitude of the Federal government. If after four years, negotiations are not underway, or progressing to Quebec's satisfaction, a referendum on whether Quebec should stay in Confederation will be held.	The Liberal Party wants to accelerate the negotiations to change the constitution in order to get a more precise, more efficient sharing of powers between the two levels of government to prevent duplication.
Unemployment	
Create upwards of 50,000 new jobs annually during the next four years and make a complete inventory of the manpower situation. Review the needs for labor of the various sectors of the economy. More than half of the current unemployment of 9.2 per cent is attributable to the federal government's anti-inflation measures.	The first priority of my government will be the untangling of our financial mess to re-allocate money, if necessary, to job-creating investments, capital expenditures (roads, Government construction, S.G.F. investment). Our unemployment rate is at an unprecedented height. It must be curbed at all costs.
Economic development	
The creation of an industrial development company to promote and attract industry to Quebec, and to oversee the merger of key industries where needed. Creation of an export information board to promote Quebec exports, and greater incentive to Quebec industries.	Economic development is as much a priority in Quebec as the creation of 100,000 new jobs. Without it, we cannot achieve our goals of solving unemployment. Development must be rational and fast. To do this we must carefully choose the priorities of our government.
Federal-Provincial	
The revision of cost-sharing programs and bringing back of all such programs to exclusive Quebec jurisdiction. The return to Quebec jurisdiction of social security programs now in federal hands. The return of the $200,000,000 collected by Ottawa in the past two years of social development tax.	The National Union has used those relations for its own electoral purposes, blaming Ottawa's riding policies towards Quebec. If Prime Minister Trudeau doesn't accept our economic federalism, he is not a true federalist and Canada's future will be in danger.

Rene Lévesque PARTI QUÉBÉCOIS	Camil Samson CRÉDITISTE
Constitution and independence	
The Parti Québécois wants Quebec to be a sovereign state – a country that will be politically independent from Canada though linked to it economically.	Quebec would take over its full responsibility for all fields which fall within its jurisdiction under the constitution. These include all direct taxation, social welfare, human rights, education and immigration. Quebec would also have control over its own financial credit. The Ralliement does not see the need for independence, we're neither federalists nor separatists – we're Créditistes.
Unemployment	
The quarrels between the Ottawa and Quebec governments aggravates unemployment. It is necessary to take the instruments of economic action into our own hands and that is the only way unemployment can be reduced in Quebec. Radical reorganization of employment officers will be undertaken.	By making money available free of interest, jobs will be created. With more wage-earners the purchase of goods will be greatly increased, this leading to stepped-up productivity, which will again cut unemployment.
Economic development	
There is no question of our denying the necessity and utility of certain economic links with the rest of Canada and the United States. Quebec will continue a good neighbor policy with Canada and the U.S. The party will establish a Department of National Economy to regroup natural resources, lands and forests, commerce and industry, tourism, fish and game.	Same as above.
Federal-Provincial	
Quebec and Canada would form two separate countries within the framework of an economic and administrative alliance on a contractual and renewable basis.	The federal system can work well, provided that Ottawa can be induced to allow the province necessary control of its credit, through the establishment of an autonomous Quebec branch of the Bank of Canada.

Jean-Jacques Bertrand NATIONAL UNION	Robert Bourassa LIBERAL
Education	
Streamlining and modernization of actual school board structures into new and more viable units. We will make CEGEP's curriculum meet the particular manpower needs of the community the CEGEP is located in. Adult retraining programs will be expanded and French will be better taught in the schools by training more and better qualified French teachers. Free education at the university level will be introduced gradually.	It's in an unbelievable mess. Parents are worried, students are disoriented, teachers are not paid. Education problems today are due to lack of leadership. We have to fit our graduates into the labor market, we need better information on possible opportunities. A Liberal government will establish permanent re-adaption centres.
French language	
We will make French the priority language in Quebec without doing away with the minority language rights in education. A linguistic research centre will be established, and the greater use of French will be promoted in industry and commerce.	French must be the working language of Quebec but we don't need to break up Canada to achieve that goal. Our approach is on the working language first, education after. If people work in French, they will send their children to the French schools.

In his relentlessly thorough way Claude Ryan surveyed the scene and made his choice in long editorials (*Le Devoir*, April 23–25). Confessing that no one could predict the results, he wrote:

... The people of Quebec must first decide whether they will vote to break the federal link with the rest of Canada or to retain this link during the next four years. They may have a thousand different reasons for supporting the Parti québécois. They should not forget that, in voting for this party, they are voting in favour of Quebec's political separation from the rest of Canada.

As Pierre Vadeboncœur says in the work mentioned yesterday, the choice between federalism and independence has become "our main political problem," "an important subject," "a crucial question." Similarly, this is how men like René Lévesque and Jacques Parizeau have put the question which must be resolved on April 29 before the electors. Henceforth this is how the problem will be seen by thousands of Québécois.

It is vital therefore that next Wednesday the people of Quebec state clearly whether they are for or against retaining the federal link as it now stands. Secondly, supposing they are in favour of retaining the federal link, they must say which of the three other parties is best suited to ensure the political development of Quebec within a Canadian framework ...

Mr Ryan himself opted for the federalist option, but felt compelled to deal at length with the Péquistes:

The case of the Parti québécois is more involved, more intricate. In its two

Rene Lévesque PARTI QUÉBÉCOIS	Camil Samson CRÉDITISTE
Education	
The school system will be free up to and including university level and a system of living allowances for students to include a pre-salary plan, will also be established.	The denominational school system will be restored as the base for the future so that everyone can have the sort of education he chooses.
French language	
French will become the only official language. A law will make the use of French obligatory in all business. But the PQ will respect the rights of English-speaking citizens who will receive grants from the government on a percentage basis of population.	French will be the priority language, but the acquired rights of the minorities will be respected. Parents will have the freedom of choice for the type of education they want for their children.

years of existence the PQ has accomplished a colossal task and rendered immeasurable service to democracy in Quebec.

This party has channelled countless sources of energy which would otherwise have been drawn into disgust, indifference, complete abstainment, or anarchy into democratic involvement. The party has acted as a voice for thousands of citizens drawn not solely from the ranks of those who favour self-determination, but also from the even larger band of those who feel the need for fundamental political renewal. In the democratic nature of its internal structure and the large public meetings which have marked the regular conventions, the party has demonstrated its belief in free discussion, democratic guidelines, and hard work. Its leader is an exceptional person who, because of his courage, his experience on the public scene, and his energy, is the strongest leader around. In the space of a few months he has succeeded in giving respect and credibility to an option which not so long ago was considered unacceptable and eccentric. And finally this party offers to the people of Quebec a team of candidates which includes at least twenty men of outstanding value.

Despite all these points in its favour – most of which are the answer to our greatest expectations, we cannot support the Parti québécois in this election. This is why:

1 The fundamental proposal put forward by the PQ, that is, Quebec's political separation from the rest of Canada, is premature. From now on the problem presents serious implications; above and beyond the mathematical outcome of April 29, this will be the principal achievement of the present campaign.

Québec-Presse, April 26, 1970

But the time is not ripe for resolving the problem in the radical and irrevocable manner suggested by the PQ ... When one considers the present state of the economy and of public finance in Quebec, it would be ill-advised to act so radically at this time.

2 The PQ's political programme contains serious gaps, as we pointed out here on April 9. The new balance of power which the party suggests between the various elements of the social body are inspired by generous considerations. However, it is more radical and far-reaching than it would seem at first sight. Both in the area of foreign and internal politics, the PQ's programme seems more like an idealistic forecast for the society of tomorrow than a collection of realistic proposals for the immediate future.

3 The team of candidates offered to the public by the PQ includes several interesting names which we would like to see in Parliament. Nevertheless this list is not as well-balanced as one might expect of a group which is asking for the power to govern. The list contains too high a proportion of overly young citizens, whose experience of life and of public affairs is limited ...

4 All in all the Parti québécois is still a very young party. Within its ranks there are men of varying, sometimes conflicting, tendencies. The personality of its leaders and of a few outstanding members has so far managed to create an impression of unity. But it woud appear that this unity rests on weak foundations. One feels that the real confrontations are still to come within this party. Until such time it is impossible to know clearly which way the PQ will eventually bend.

Only a few years will be needed for this filtration – or, if you like, symbiosis – to occur.

Dismissing the New Democratic party (à regret) and the Ralliement créditiste, Mr Ryan observed: "If we were to go along with a conventional wisdom which has on occasion been overlooked at great cost to Quebec, this time we should come down on the side of the Union nationale. By so doing we would avoid having a "rouge" government in Ottawa and a "rouge" government in Quebec. The ever-present risk of alliances between the members of the same political family would be circumscribed." But conventional wisdom had to be shelved, he concluded, because the Union nationale "does not possess the language, the analytical or working methods which suit younger generations or the new technocratical élite who have been trained in the modern governmental sciences." Only the Liberals remained:

... The Liberal party chief, Mr Bourassa, has not offered the public the outstanding team he promised at the time of his leadership campaign. He appears before the public at the head of a party which for four years has seemed to be vacillating after the enthusiasm which it initially showed for a truer democratization. He has not answered all the questions which needed to be on certain key aspects of his programme, notably in respect of the promise of 100,000 new jobs in 1971. He has not yet given sufficient guarantee that he will be firm in possible negotiations with the central government.

And yet, of the three leaders representing those parties which are inclined to give federalism a serious chance, he has appeared as the one most capable of taking the struggle into enemy territory, of entering into dialogue with young people, of tackling and understanding problems with the technical ability required in our time of a man of state. Furthermore he has appeared as the man who is surrounded for the time being by a team of moderate youthfulness, representing various areas of activity ...

Constitutionally speaking the Liberal party has not given definite replies to the criticisms levelled against it during the campaign. But Mr Bourassa has shown no degree of servility in so far as Ottawa is concerned. In terms which may be too concise but which are down to earth, he has stipulated those attitudes which differentiate him quite clearly from the Trudeau team. He has not tied his hands for the future. When one remembers that – to spur him on – he will have not only the Union nationale but also the Parti québécois, the risk he might present in different circumstances is considerably lessened. Once prime minister, Mr Bourassa will be well-advised (as will the rest of Canada) to see that federalism operates in accordance with the fundamental expectations of Quebec.

Of the three parties with federalist tendencies, the Liberal party also seems to be the one most capable of bringing about an economic upsurge and at the same time the rationalization of public administration of which Quebec stands so much in need. Mr Bourassa possesses an excellent understanding of the mechanics of economic activity and public administration in North America. He understands the language of figures. Without any hesitation he admits the necessity for private enterprise and at the same time is fully acquainted with the new forms that the state's intervention in the economy takes in our time. We have more confidence, for the immediate future, in his approach, than in the Union nationale's improvisations or in Messrs Parizeau's or Lévesque's overconfident equations ...

The Verdict

"Today this feels like a splendid country," shouted the *Globe and Mail* on April 30, for "the Province of Quebec is alive and well in Canada." More soberly the *Montreal Star* assured its up-tight English-Canadian readers that "Quebec has granted us a second chance." The *Gazette* saw the Liberal victory as "a vote of confidence in Canada." "Quebec voters respond in a fashion reassuring to Canadians in all parts of the country," echoed the *Winnipeg Free Press*. On the surface, at least, the electoral verdict seemed to justify such optimistic conclusions (1966 figures are bracketed):

	Seats	Percentage of total vote
Liberals	72 (50)	41.8 (47)
Parti québécois	7	23
Union nationale	17 (56)	19.6 (41)
Ralliement créditiste	12	11.1
Others	0 (2)	4.5 (12)

Globe and Mail, Toronto, April 30, 1970

The federalist rejoicing was understandable, but overdone. For the Liberal sweep alone did nothing to remove the serious economic and social problems; and in it were seeds of further antagonisms and potentially dangerous political reorganization.

"In giving you their support," wired Mr Trudeau to Mr Bourassa, "it is clear that the people of Quebec have accepted your option: the path of work, of reason, and of confidence." It was equally clear, however, that the Liberal share of the popular vote declined sharply, despite the obvious increase in the turnout of English-speaking or non-French Quebeckers. Far clearer was that a troubled and discontented electorate had gone to the polls on April 29. Never strong in the cities, the Union nationale was virtually wiped out by the urban voters. Rural malaise found its outlet in a massive swing to the Ralliement créditiste, which won nine seats from the Union nationale and three from the Liberals. Moreover, in fourteen additional UN seats the Créditistes, often running second to the victorious Liberals, gave Bourassa the seat by attracting thousands of UN supporters.

For several years before the 1970 election students of Quebec separatism had pointed out that a significant fraction – sometimes estimated at 50 per cent – of nationalists espousing the separatist cause simply felt that Mr Lévesque was a better leader than his opponents or that the Parti québécois had a domestic programme better suited to the needs of Quebec society. Pre-election polls revealed much the same thing. Undoubtedly that programme was designed to appeal to the urban voter, and whether it was nationalism or radicalism that was so appealing, the Parti québécois made a remarkable showing in urban Quebec. In Montreal's depressed east end it swept five seats from the Union nationale and one from the Liberals. Elsewhere in the city it ran second to the Liberals in every riding, including the Anglophone areas. Excluding the four overwhelmingly English constituencies, the Liberals secured only 373,757 votes to 249,251 for the Parti québécois. To the north and south of Montreal, it often ran a strong second, and lost Fabre by only ninety-one votes. In more than twenty-five constituencies outside Montreal the Parti québécois polled more than one-fifth of the vote, showing signs of real strength in Quebec City, the depressed lower south shore, and the north – where it won Saguenay from the Liberals and ran second in Lac St-Jean and Jonquière. Only in the highly overrepresented rural counties southeast of Montreal and in the areas bordering Ontario did it show little strength.

Federalists and English Canadians observed that seven out of ten voters had rejected the separatist solution. Including the Union nationale as resolutely federalist (despite its ambiguous position on the constitutional future) the conclusion was as accurate as election generalizations can be. Separatist analysts were not content with such gross statistics, however. Even on election night it was clear that English-speaking Quebec had voted solidly Liberal. The charges that Mr Bourassa owed his majority to English-speaking Quebec – and that Mr Lévesque had been defeated by the Anglophones in Laurier – were repeated in the days that passed, and were finally argued with statistical documentation in Bernard Smith's *Le Coup d''Etat du Avril 29* (which appeared in the autumn).

Breaking the City of Montreal and a number of other constituencies down by percentage of French Canadians and non-French Canadians, and also breaking the constituencies down into areas ranging from 80 to 90 per cent to 0 to 10 per cent non-French Canadian, Mr Smith easily demonstrated that English Canadians had voted Liberal and that the gap between the Liberals and the Parti québécois often varied with the percentage of non-French Canadians in the constituency. Only in nine of the thirty-eight seats in Montreal and its environs, Smith's figures argued, did the Liberals secure a higher percentage of the French-Cana-

Québec-Presse, May 3, 1970

dian vote than the Péquistes. (One was Mercier, where Bourassa secured an estimated three hundred more French-Canadian votes than his opponent Pierre Bourgault, but emerged with a comfortable margin of more than three thousand thanks to a solid English vote.) Taking the province as a whole Smith concluded that French-speaking Quebec had given 32.6 per cent of its support to the Liberals, 28.7 to the PQ, 24.2 to the UN, and 14.5 per cent to others. The decision in twenty ridings, he declared, was determined by the non-French-Canadian vote. The conclusion was clear: without those twenty seats the Liberals in the National Assembly would have been in a minority, as they were in the popular vote.

Never before in modern Quebec's history had the line between many French Canadians and the non-French Canadians been so firmly and clearly drawn, unless it was the provincial election of 1939. The conflicts over separatism, and perhaps equally over language and educational policy, had born fruit. The issue was personalized and the results more bitter on election night when it was clear that the Italian-Canadian voters of Laurier had deserted Lévesque and refused to give their support to an Italian UN candidate to vote solidly Liberal, and that in Ahuntsic non-French Canadians had narrowly defeated Jacques Parizeau. Commenting on the Brinks affair and the joyful reactions in Montreal's English dailies, Mr Parizeau warned that "these people are just waving a red flag in front of a fuming bull ... they are really asking for trouble." Not only were the internal tensions made more acute, but the election results led many to question the democratic or representative system. As Parizeau exclaimed: "God help us ... You see it is not my defeat nor that of René Lévesque that is important ... It's the defeat of our arguments in favour of the parliamentary system."

While some ultra-nationalists were prepared to spend four years strengthening the PQ base and preparing for the predictable takeover in the next election, others were not. René Lévesque himself cautioned moderation and claimed an immense victory on election night, but by August his tone was different in an interview with the Canadian Press (*Ottawa Citizen*, August 22):

Q: How do you interpret the election results? Some saw massive approval for federalism in the election.

A: First a fact that is terribly flagrant. It's that 95 per cent of the Anglophone bloc – I studied enough polls, including Laurier – voted Liberal ... Even little old ladies on stretchers were hauled out in the end-of-régime panic, as if it were the end of the Roman Empire. They got them out and they manipulated them to the hilt ...

There's another striking thing about the election. It's that the defeated candidates we are most sorry about, men like Parizeau and Morin ... were often defeated only by the vote of the Anglophone ghetto. They had bigger French majorities ... than those who were elected. In other words they got a bigger percentage of the French vote than those who won. That's the disturbing second fact considered from the point of view of the possibilities of the democratic process.

Is Montreal going to be annexed sufficiently year after year to make it impossible for the majority group in Quebec to win an increasing number of ridings at Montreal? This is the danger of assimilation, which is increasing. The electoral map will figure in this. We'll see what kind of work will be done in reforming the map. But you know things could get pretty damned serious if the will, becoming clearer and clearer of an ethnic majority, is blocked by an ethnic minority within Quebec.

I don't have to draw pictures for you. It can become very grave ... in other countries this kind of thing provokes explosions.

Q: Has your attitude towards Quebec's English-speaking minority changed since the election?

A: I want to be very clear about this ... I know very well that your interview will be reproduced honestly. That happens once every six months in a sort of sea of propaganda organized by your English mass media. That doesn't change things very much. It's the typical good old Anglo-Saxon method: "Let's give him a day in court."

I'm not talking about you. I'm talking about those who manipulate your information and your propaganda in the English media. I was brought up half in English and half in French and have lived in English as much as I have lived in French. Yet I have never experienced such disgust ... as the disgust I experienced because of the way information was manipulated in the Anglo-Saxon Establishment at Montreal with its propaganda media, its disrespect for a population which is treated like "natives."

Q: Can the independence of Quebec really be achieved democratically? Considering the makeup of the population and the electoral map, it seems that the answer is no.

A: It's possible eventually that the answer will be no. It's possible only we can't accept it ... I think that the last democratic chance will be in the next election ... And if there is the same manipulation of elections – and I'm talking more about manipulation of the minds than of the electoral system – it's obvious that the conscious minority ... is going to have the almost irresistible temptation to blow up the institutions. But I honestly believe there is still a chance.

The Cross Abduction

OCTOBER 5–10

AT 8:15 on Monday morning, October 5, two armed men pushed past the maid at 1297 Redpath Crescent in Westmount. Within minutes James Richard Cross, senior British trade commissioner in Montreal, had dressed under the barrel of a sub-machine gun and been whisked away in a taxi. The Montreal police had difficulty understanding the garbled plea for help from the Cross' Greek maid, and by the time they arrived on Redpath Crescent Jasper Cross, as he was known, had disappeared without a trace. Strangely enough the kidnapping took the nation by surprise, strangely because the disappearance of James Cross had been foretold in almost a decade of the activities of the Front de libération du Québec.

Towards October

The escalation of revolutionary activity in Quebec late in 1969 seemed forgotten in the early months of 1970. In English Canada, and often in Quebec itself, the overt signs of continued FLQ activity were overlooked completely or buried as minor news items in the inside pages of the paper. Freed on $2,500 bail, put up by the Confederation of National Trade Unions (CNTU), on February 20, Charles Gagnon, an FLQ leader charged with homicide, immediately held a press conference and declared that he planned to revive the FLQ at once and make it the most representative movement of the revolutionary forces in Quebec to destroy "the fascist and racist power that we know in North America." In his speaking tour Mr Gagnon appealed for solidarity with the Palestinian liberation struggle; and later, joined by Stanley Gray, president of the Front de libération populaire, and Louis-Philippe Aubert, former Company of Young Canadians (CYC) volunteer and head of the St Henri workers committee, both CNTU organizers, he organized a Committee for Solidarity with the Black Panthers. Pierre Vallières, author of the FLQ bible, *Nègres blancs d'Amérique*, was freed on bail on May 26, the money again being secured by the CNTU. The two men had become heros of the

Québec-Presse, July 12, 1970

FLQ and the New Left, their long trials publicizing the radical revolutionary movement and, to some, giving an air of credibility to the term "political prisoners."

While the Gagnon-Vallières team attracted considerable public attention, other members of the FLQ worked less openly. On February 26 Montreal police stopped a rented panel truck and found two men, arms, a large wicker basket, and a document announcing that the FLQ had just kidnapped Moshe Golan, the Israeli consul and trade commissioner in Montreal. The men, Jacques Lanctôt and Pierre Marcil, were charged with conspiracy to kidnap and released on bail. Lanctôt disappeared. Another group, led by Robert and Gabriel Hudon, both free on parole from earlier FLQ convictions, were busily engaged in raising funds, presumably for FLQ operations but also it appeared for Robert Hudon's personal pleasure. Before the gang was arrested it had carried out more than two dozen robberies. The leading "soldier" of the robbery group, Marc-Andre Gagné (Lavoie) deserted in March and was later arrested. The Hudon brothers and Pierre Demers were arrested in June. (According to Gustave Morf in *Terror in Quebec*, the Hudon group planned an abortive attempt in February to kidnap Gagnon, Robert Lemieux, the radical separatist lawyer who had acted for many members of the FLQ, and Jacques Larue-Langlois, a former Radio-Canada producer, for monopolizing FLQ statements before the media.)

Late in May the FLQ resumed its familiar pattern of bombings. On May 24 a powerful bomb exploded at the entrance of the former Montreal Board of Trade office in the financial district, shattering windows for two blocks. Four days later bombs exploded outside the doctors' residence at Queen Mary's Veterans Hospital and the General Electric Plant, and as police checked, the University of Montreal Students' Union was robbed of $58,000, presumably by an FLQ cell. Five bombs rocked Westmount on Sunday, May 31, four of them at private homes. Two others were dismantled.

On June 2 a woman who had rented her garage to two men found a cache of dynamite, two machine guns, hoods, and a bullet-proof vest. That evening another four hundred sticks of dynamite were stolen, some of which may have gone into the bombs that exploded at Le Club Canadien on June 5 and on the McGill campus ten days later. Following a tip to radio station CKAC, police defused two other bombs on June 15 outside IBM and the Domtar Research Centre. On the night of June 17–18 a bomb shattered the windows of a post office in Longueuil, and a letter from the FLQ a few days later claimed credit. Describing Postmaster-

General Eric Kierans as "anti-union," the letter stated that the FLQ would continue to show their support for the Lapalme workers until they were re-hired. The letter was accompanied by an FLQ manifesto in which the group said it was simply responding to

... psychological terrorism and to the blackmail of businessmen who believe they can maintain the present political and economic structures by spreading the fear of change among the population.

To bombs of the Royal Trust type we are in true opposition. We can only respond to their violence with counter-violence. We are defending ourselves against permanent attacks of anti-worker and anti-Quebec forces which are the financial syndicates, the chambers of commerce, the huge industries, and others, who are sustained by the Liberal party of Trudeau-Bourassa.

Although his family was at home, no one was hurt on June 19 when another bomb hit the home of financier Jean-Louis Lévesque.

Meanwhile, on June 1 Justice Minister Jérôme Choquette had announced a $50,000 reward for information leading to the arrest of the bombers, and a week later formed a high-powered committee of the Quebec Provincial Police, the Montreal police, and the RCMP to coordinate anti-terrorist activities. The reward apparently paid off, for a tip led police to a summer home in the Laurentians, near Prévost, and a house in suburban Laval. At Prévost the police arrested four people and seized three hundred pounds of dynamite, clocks and detonators, hoods, rifles, revolvers and ammunition, $28,000 in cash (presumably from the university robbery), and tracts calling for a revolution of Quebec workers. More dynamite was found in Laval, where two were arrested. Also located at Prévost was an FLQ communiqué announcing the kidnapping of the American consul in Montreal and listing the "irrevocable conditions" for his life: the release of all "political prisoners" and their transportation to Cuba; reinstatement of the "revolutionary Lapalme workers"; the payment of "a voluntary tax of $500,000 in gold ingots"; broadcasting and publication of all FLQ communiqués; and the end of all police investigations and arrests. The selection of an American seemed to be symbolic:

By the kidnapping of Consul Burgess the FLQ wants to stress its revolutionary solidarity with all those countries which fight against the economic, social, and cultural domination of the Americans in the world. This means unconditional support of the movements in Latin America and Palestine, support of the American blacks and of all the peoples of Africa and Asia who work for their liberation.

The FLQ thus aligns itself with the Cuban stand which vigorously denounces American imperialism and which promises to support all those fighting against that hegemony. The political prisoners will surely be able to benefit from the extraordinary experience of the Cubans, whom we want to thank in advance for the concern they will show to our comrades the political prisoners.

Long live the Cuban people!

Long live Fidel!

Long live the Cuban revolution!

Accompanying the communiqué was a manifesto to be read on radio and television, and published in all major newspapers.

Brought before the Quebec Fire Commissioner, Cyrille Delage, who was investigating the bombings, were: André Roy, 23, an unemployed taxi driver, and his wife Nicole, 26; Pierre Carrier, 30, unemployed; Maude Martin, 26, script assistant at Radio-Canada and Carrier's girl friend; Claude Morency, 19, unemployed; and François Lanctôt, 21, a labourer and brother of Jacques Lanctôt. On the following day, with lawyers Bernard Mergler and Robert Lemieux on hand, the four men refused to testify "before the representatives of the establishment, that is, St James Street, the Westmount bourgeosie, and the Outremont bourgeosie," as Mr Roy said, and were jailed for refusing to testify. The police declared that the bomb materials at Prévost were identical to those dismantled in Westmount on May 31.

The breakup of another cell did not stop the bombing. At 3:45 AM on June 22, four hours after the arrests were announced, another terrorist bomb ripped open a bank in Tracy, near Sorel. At 6:25 AM on June 24, St Jean Baptiste day, an anonymous caller advised Ottawa radio station CKOY that a bomb would explode in one minute. At 6:28 a ten-to-twelve stick dynamite bomb exploded outside the Department of National Defence "B" Building, killing Mrs Jeanne D'Arc St Germain, a communications supervisor, and injuring two soldiers. In a June 30 letter to the media, the FLQ hardly surprised police by claiming responsibility for the explosion. On July 12 a Volkswagen, laden with 150 pounds of fused dynamite, was found outside the Bank of Montreal on St James Street and defused before it exploded and demolished the building and others around it. Two days later Mr Choquette rushed an explosion control bill through the National Assembly, stating that the upsurge of terrorism was not connected with separatism but was due to "ideological elements of foreign inspiration ... which have no support among our population." The bill had little effect. The autumn saw a wave of dynamite thefts, more than three thousand sticks having been reported as stolen in August and September.

Meanwhile, the recently formed Mouvement pour la défense des prisonniers politiques had opposed the new bill as placing too much power in the

Québec-Presse, July 5, 1970

hands of police. The movement had been established to raise $50,000 for the defence of the terrorists, a sum symbolically the same as that provided by the government for information. The committee was headed by Dr Serge Mongeau, a PQ candidate in the April election; Gaston Miron, a poet and publisher; and Guy Marsolais, a senior official of the CNTU. Interviewed by Ronald Lebel (*Globe Magazine*, September 19), Jacques Larue-Langlois, a spokesman for the movement, said:

> Choquette is trying to create a new national hero in Quebec – the stool pigeon. We want to open a national campaign against police informers. We also want to apply public pressure on the Quebec newspaper monopolies like Power Corporation to publish the statements put out by the FLQ.
>
> We want to improve the image of those who have decided to move into action in the liberation struggle of the Québécois people, so that the public will understand the political dimensions of the bombs. The reaction we want when a bomb goes off is an immense "Bravo!" not comments like "Isn't it sickening."

Tired of the endless bombings and the rhetoric of the FLQ, Canadians dismissed the plot to kidnap the Israeli and American consuls without a passing glance. Even an experienced reporter like Mr Lebel, commenting on the Burgess note, admitted that the Montreal police took it all seriously but observed that "There is a temptation to scoff at this kind of purple-red prose." Scoffing ceased on October 5.

The FLQ Demands

The kidnapping of a foreign diplomat immediately brought the federal government directly into the crisis posed by the FLQ. In Ottawa, the second floor of the East Block became the headquarters of a task force, which established a network of lines to maintain direct communication with Quebec, Montreal, the commercial news services, the Prime Minister's Office and residence, and Canadian missions abroad. Selected to speak for the government, Mitchell Sharp, secretary of state for external affairs, made a brief statement in the Commons at 2:40 that afternoon (October 5):

> Mr. Speaker, I regret to have to inform the House that Mr. James Richard Cross, Senior Trade Commissioner of the British Trade Commission in Montreal, was abducted from his home early this morning by armed men. The reasons for this act have not been conclusively established. Police were immediately informed and road blocks and spot checks on major arteries leading to and from the city, including bridges leading to the south shore, have been established. The Montreal Police, the Quebec Provincial Police and the RCMP are co-operating in investigating this case.
>
> The Canadian government is consulting closely with the British authorities in this matter. It is fully aware of its responsibility for the protection of foreign

representatives in this country and is sparing no effort to discharge this duty. All appropriate steps are being taken to ensure additional protection for diplomatic and consular persons and premises. We are in close touch with all provincial and municipal authorities concerned and there is no doubt as to their full co-operation.

By that time the government knew more, for at 11:45 radio station CKAC in Montreal had been informed by an anonymous caller, the communication system the FLQ cells were to use, that documents had been left at the Lafontaine Pavilion. Police and reporters arrived at the same time, and the following communiqué was found. Its contents were immediately placed before the Quebec and Canadian governments, but the communiqué was not broadcast until 9:30 the next morning:

The representative of Great Britain in Quebec, Mr J. Cross, is in the hands of the Front de libération du Québec.

Here are the conditions that the ruling authorities must fulfil in order to save the life of the representative of the ancient racist and colonialist British system.

1 They must see to it that the repressive police forces do not commit the monstrous error of attempting to jeopardize the success of the operation by conducting searches, investigations, raids, arrests by any other means.

2 The political manifesto which the Front de libération du Québec will address to the ruling authorities must appear in full on the front page of all the principal newspapers in Quebec. The ruling authorities, after consulting with the latter, must make public the list of Quebec newspapers agreeing to publish our manifesto. But it should be quite clear that all Quebec regions must be covered.

Furthermore, this manifesto must be read in full and commented upon by the political prisoners before their departure during a programme, the length of which will have to be at least thirty minutes, to be televised live or pre-recorded between 8 and 11 PM on Radio-Canada and its affiliated stations in the province.

3 Liberation of political prisoners: Cyriaque Delisle, Edmond Guénette and François Schirm, Serge Demers, Marcel Faulkner, Gérard Laquerre, Robert Lévesque, Réal Mathieu, and Claude Simard; Pierre-Paul Geoffroy, Michel Loriot, Pierre Demers, Gabriel Hudon, Robert Hudon, Marc-André Gagné, François Lanctôt, Claude Morency, and André Roy; Pierre Boucher and André Ouellette (recently re-arrested by the police of Drapeau-the-Dog).

Wives and children of the political prisoners must be allowed to join them if they so desire.

Furthermore, political prisoners André Lessard, Pierre Marcil, and Réjean Tremblay, presently out on bail, must be allowed to join their patriotic comrades and leave Quebec if they so desire.

4 A plane must be made available to the patriotic political prisoners for their transport to either Cuba or Algeria, once an official agreement has been reached with one of these two countries.

Furthermore, they must be allowed to be accompanied by their respective lawyers and by at least two political reporters of two French Quebec dailies.

front de libération du québec

communiqué

opération libération

Le représentant de la [illegible] au Québec, M. J. Cross est entre les mains du [illegible] du québec.

Voi[illegible] les conditons que [illegible] en place devront remplir pour [illegible]server la vie au [illegible] vieux sytème britannique, [illegible] et coloni[illegible].

1. Elles devront veiller à ce que les forces policières répressives ne commet[illegible] monstrueuse de tenter de compromettre le succès de l'opération en faisant fouilles, recherches, perquisitions, ar[illegible] ou tous autres stratagèmes.

2. Le manifeste p[illegible] que fera parvenir aux autorités en place le Front de Libéra[illegible] Québec devra paraître intégralement en première page de tous les grands journaux du Québec. Les autorités en place devront, après consultations avec ceux-ci, nous faire connaître publiquement la liste des journaux québécois qui acceptent de publier notre manifeste. Mais qu'il soit bien clair que toutes les régions du Québec devront être couvertes.

5 During a meeting attended by the Lapalme boys and the Postmaster-General – or a representative – the latter must promise to reinstate them. The reinstatement promise must take into account the standards and conditions already secured by the revolutionary workers of Lapalme prior to the breaking off of negotiations. This meeting must be held within forty-eight hours after the release of this communiqué and must be open to newsmen.

6 A voluntary tax of $500,000 in gold bullion must be put aboard the plane made available to the political prisoners. When one recalls the spendings caused

by the recent visit of the Queen of England, the millions of dollars lost by the Post Office Department because of the stubborn millionaire Kierans, the cost of maintaining Quebec within Confederation, etc. ... $500,000 is peanuts!

7 The NAME and the PICTURE of the informer who led police to the last FLQ cell must be made public and published. The Front de libération du Québec is in possession of information dealing with the acts and moves of this louse ... and is only awaiting "official" confirmation to act.

Through this move, the Front de libération du Québec wants to draw the attention of the world to the fate of French-speaking Québécois, a majority which is jeered at and crushed on its own territory by a faulty political system (Canadian federalism) and by an economy dominated by the interests of American high finance, the racist and imperialist "big bosses."

When you examine the origins of Confederation you are in a better position to understand what were the true interests ($ $ $) which inspired those who were called the Fathers of Confederation. Besides, in 1867, the Quebec people (Lower Canada) were not consulted as to the possibility of creating a Confederation of existing provinces. It was a question of big money and these questions are only sorted out by interested parties, the capitalists, those who possess and amass capital and the means of production and who, according to their sole needs and requirements decide on our whole lives as well as those of a race of people.

Thousands of Québécois have understood, as did our ancestors of 1837–38, that the only way to ensure our national as well as economic survival is total independence.

The Front de libération du Québec supports unconditionally the American blacks and those of Africa, the liberation movements of Latin America, of Palestine, and of Asia, the revolutionary Catholics of Northern Ireland and all those who fight for their freedom, their independence, and their dignity.

The Front de libération du Québec wants to salute the Cuban and Algerian people who are heroically fighting against imperialism and colonialism in all its forms, for a just society where man's exploitation by man is banished.

However, we believe that the only really true support we can give these people moving towards their liberations is to liberate ourselves first. During and after our struggle we shall offer much more than the usual sympathy of shocked intellectuals confronted with pictures showing aggression in a peaceful and blissful setting.

Here is how the various steps must be carried out:

1 As soon as this communiqué is received by the ruling authorities, they must immediately free all the aforementioned political prisoners and take them to the Montreal International Airport. There, a private room must be placed at their disposal straightaway so they can fraternize and become acquainted with the manifesto, the conditions outlined as well as the steps of the operation. A full copy of the manifesto and of this communiqué must be given to them.

2 They must undergo no harm, brutality, torture, or blackmail.

3 In the hours following the liberation of the political prisoners, a room must be turned into a studio where they will be able to:

Communicate with their respective lawyers;

Make a public announcement of their personal decision. The political prisoners can accept or refuse to leave Quebec; in other words, the imprisoned patriots are allowed to dissent in view of the disparity between the sentences imposed upon each of them;

Read and discuss the manifesto during a televised and broadcast programme, as set out earlier in the conditions;

Meet all the friends and militants who may wish to go and see them.

4 The ruling authorities must ensure the return to Montreal of legal advisers and newsmen who will accompany the political prisoners to Cuba or Algeria.

5 The "voluntary tax" of $500,000 in gold bullion must be taken to Dorval airport in nine BRINKS trucks. If this raises any technical problem, the authorities can surely call upon the "experts" who managed to make such a brilliant get-away at the time of the now famous "Brink's show" on the eve of the election. Newsmen (including the one from the *Gazette* just like in the good old days) must be allowed to attend the departure and arrival of the "happy group."

All these conditions and their fulfilment must be dealt with within forty-eight hours from the release of this communiqué. All these conditions are irrevocable. The life of the diplomat depends therefore on the good-will of the ruling authorities.

Once the Front de libération du Québec has made sure that the lawyers and newsmen are on their way back and the latter have confirmed the arrival of the political prisoners as well as the voluntary tax which must be checked by Cuban or Algerian experts, and once they have confirmed that everything went according to plan, then and then only will the diplomat be set free.

We feel confident that the imprisoned political patriots will benefit from the experience in Cuba or Algiers and we thank them in advance for the concern which they will express for our Quebec comrades.

We shall overcome!

Front de libération du Québec.

While Ottawa and Quebec studied the FLQ demands the kidnappers prepared another communiqué. The exact nature of the document and its discovery remain uncertain; but according to Lucien Rivard (*La Presse*, October 7) it was delivered to CKAC by taxi at 6 PM. As reprinted in *La Presse* the first page of the document seemed to be an appeal to the media:

The health of Mr Cross is excellent. Everyone, including his wife, can be reassured. Besides, Mr Cross has written to his wife and the letter was deposited in a mailbox at the corner of Sherbrooke and Victor-Bourgeau streets.

We have notified the central council of the CSN [Confédération des syndicats nationaux] about this letter.

We call upon your co-operation as media agents to break the wall of silence that the fascist police have erected around the liberation operation by systematically stealing all of the communiqués and our manifesto which were destined to the various information media.

The second page of the communiqué, which seemed to Mr Rivard to have been drafted separately, was aimed at the government. The text was released by Mr Choquette at a press conference the following morning:

Front de libération du Québec, Communiqué no 2, October 6, 1970, 12 noon, deadline: 24 hours.

The present authorities do not seem to take seriously the recommendations put forward by the Front de libération du Québec in the first communiqué.

In order to save the life of the diplomat Cross, it would be wiser to meet our conditions than to make melodramatic appeals about pills that J. Cross must take.

Let it be clearly understood that when the time limit has passed we will not hesitate at all to liquidate J. Cross ... because the life and liberty of the political prisoners and of the Lapalme guys are well worth hundreds of diplomats serving only the financial interests of the Anglo-Saxon and American big bosses. The present authorities alone will be truly responsible for his death.

WE SHALL OVERCOME

FRONT DE LIBERATION DU QUEBEC

Remark 1 – The contents of this communiqué must absolutely be made public.
Remark 2 – We enclose with this second communiqué a letter by J. Cross to his wife.

The Government Replies

Meanwhile in Ottawa the Prime Minister arrived on Parliament Hill early on the morning of October 6. Following his regular briefing by Gordon Robertson and Marc Lalonde, he met the inner cabinet – Sharp, Benson, Jean Marchand, Charles Drury, Donald Macdonald, Don Jamieson, and Arthur Laing – joined for the occasion by George McIlraith, the minister responsible for the RCMP. Apparently a decision was reached to reject the demands, a conclusion discussed with Mr Bourassa and British Prime Minister Edward Heath. That afternoon the Prime Minister sat briefly in the Commons, providing non-communicative answers to opposition questions. The full cabinet met later for two hours and presumably ratified the earlier decision. With most MPs and their wives attending a reception at the Prime Minister's residence, Mr Sharp made a statement to an almost empty House after the dinner recess. After summarizing the FLQ demands, he declared:

The communiqué demands that these conditions be met within 48 hours from the time of the issuing of the communiqué. Clearly, these are wholly unreasonable demands and their authors could not have expected them to be accepted. I need hardly say that this set of demands will not be met. I continue, however, to hope that some basis can be found for Mr. Cross's safe return. Indeed, I hope the abductors will find a way to establish communication to achieve this. All the authorities concerned are dealing with this case on the basis that we have the double responsibility to do our best to safeguard Mr. Cross and at the same time to preserve the rule of law in our country. The House can be sure that everything possible is being done. I trust that hon. members will not ask me to go into this delicate matter further at this moment.

The same evening in Quebec, Prime Minister Bourassa indicated that the provincial government endorsed the stand taken by Mr Sharp. "After much consultation," he said, "both levels of government agreed that the whole of the demands was too excessive and not acceptable." Meanwhile in Montreal, Robert Lemieux, who had acted for many of the criminals whose release was demanded by the FLQ, had been in touch with his clients. At a press conference on the night of October 6, Mr Lemieux declared that he believed the life of Mr Cross was in danger unless the demands were met immediately. In his boisterous manner he also attacked M. J. A. C. Lafrenière, the regional director of federal penitentiaries, whom he accused of having prevented him from seeing some of his clients, and for good measure mocked the "cité-libristes," those great defenders of civil liberties – Trudeau, Pelletier, and Marchand.

As the second deadline of noon on October 7 approached, Justice Minister Choquette issued the following appeal to the kidnappers at an 11:15 press conference:

I wish to express to Mrs Cross on behalf of the Government of the Province of Quebec and of its people the deep sympathy which we have for her following the abduction of her husband and the threat of death against him.

What is this all about? This is the case of an innocent individual who bears no responsibility whatsoever for our internal problems and who is held as hostage. It is the most serious type of blackmail which exists.

The government and the people of Quebec are scandalized. The numerous communications received by me in the last few days have been unanimous. The people reject absolutely and categorically the institution of a régime of violence and murder.

The people will realize that not only are these methods of an extremely serious nature but that they foreshadow a political system composed of odious totalitarianism, the destruction of social order which guarantees freedom, and the disappearance of lawful justice.

But then there is the case of Mr Cross as a human being. The governments are ready to investigate all practical means out of this impasse. This is the reason why I held myself available all day yesterday and last night at my office. I will continue to make myself available again today and tonight. Although, as president of the Legislation Committee of the Cabinet, I must be in Quebec this afternoon for an important meeting, the telephone in my office may be reached at all times and I can be contacted at extremely short notice. Furthermore, I will return to my office at seven o'clock this evening.

I urgently appeal to those who hold Mr Cross that they allow their respect for human life to overcome their political aspirations, misdirected as they may be. They should realize that this manner of defending their cause can only bring about its eventual defeat.

The cell responded promptly. Somewhere in the east end of Montreal at 1:30 a cabbie was given an envelope for station CKLM. The envelope contained a communiqué labelled no 4 – the third had apparently been sent to the Cross home and was not made public – a letter from Cross, and another letter from Cross to his wife. The communiqué and the public letter from Cross read:

The FLQ has decided to grant a twenty-four-hour extension to the present authorities to allow them to show their good faith. This extension will thus expire Thursday, October 8, at twelve o'clock (noon). As proof of their good faith, we demand of the present authorities:

1 Broadcasting in full of the FLQ manifesto (Communiqué no 1) by Radio-Canada. This programme must be scheduled by the television and radio networks any time between 8 PM and 11 PM. The manifesto could be read by a responsible reporter, for example, C. J. Devirieux.

2 An immediate end to all searches, raids, or arrests by the repressive police forces.

We will consider any refusal to go along with these first demands as evidence of bad faith. We will then no longer have any choice.

Rest assured, as far as we are concerned, that we will not endanger the life of the diplomat J. Cross for a question of dollars.

We shall overcome.

Front de libération du Québec.

Tuesday, 9:45 PM

1 I ask the authorities to respond favourably to the demands of the FLQ.

2 It will be faster and easier for everyone if all the FLQ communiqués are published in full.

3 Please assure that I am well and receiving the medicaments for my blood pressure.

4 I am being well treated but the FLQ are determined to achieve their demands.

J. Cross

In the House that afternoon John Diefenbaker extracted from the Prime Minister the brief comment that "hope still exists" for Mr Cross, but he was unable to determine whether the government planned to offer a reward for information leading to the arrest of the kidnappers. In answer to Eldon Woolliams' question whether the government had decided to leave the negotiations to the Quebec government, Mr Trudeau replied "No." In Montreal, Mr Lemieux declared that the authorities should stop making "vague and incautious" declarations and appoint a neutral intermediary, such as Claude Ryan or Pierre Pascau of CKLM, to negotiate with the kidnappers. At 10 PM Mr Sharp read an official statement on the media in English and French:

I have seen the text of the latest communiqué from the abductors of Mr Cross together with a letter from Mr Cross. Both the communiqué and the letter attached particular importance to the broadcasting of a certain manifesto or communiqué on radio and television over Radio-Canada. We are

Ottawa Citizen, October 7, 1970

prepared to arrange for the broadcast, although we are not quite sure which document is involved. But we must have assurances that, without the imposition of unacceptable conditions, Mr Cross will be delivered safe and sound.

I have already made clear that the set of seven conditions originally stipulated by the abductors is wholly unreasonable. What the Government needs now is the precise basis on which it can be assured of Mr Cross's safe release, and where and when. Otherwise there can be no dependable discussion since the captors might hold on to Mr Cross indefinitely. For this purpose and for the discussion of any other matters that may arise, the problem of arranging some acceptable means of communication with the abductors still remains. There are a variety of ways in which this could be done. But as a first step, I invite those holding Mr Cross to name some person with whom the authorities or a person representing the authorities can deal with confidence in making arrangements leading to Mr Cross's early and safe release.

By Wednesday the press was ready to advise the governments on the course it should pursue. From the outset Claude Ryan of *Le Devoir* favoured negotiations. But Jean-Paul Desbiens of *La Presse* (October 6) took a harder line that the paper was to follow throughout the crisis and which was more typical of Quebec press reaction than Ryan's stand:

> ... Therefore this is why it is clear that neither the municipal government, the provincial government, nor the federal government should at any time give in to this blackmail. I don't mind if they appear to be giving in, on condition that they are sure of catching the malefactors. But they must simply not give in to the basic demands behind this blackmail. We have already discussed this in connection with the bombs which exploded in the night between 30 and 31 May last, and we repeat: there is something even more disgusting than blackmail and that is to give into blackmail ...
>
> ... I am not particularly enamoured of this society; more specifically, I should say that I am not particularly enamoured of our civilization; the fact remains that I am not its elected guardian. The elected guardians of this society do not have the right to venture into the path of concessions to terrorism. If they want to give in to anything at all, they would be better off if they handed power over to the FLQ straightaway. We know they won't do this. In any case it is difficult to see how the FLQ could take over. The choice to be made by the guardians of our society is therefore clear: hold on to it; look after it. May the best man win! ...
>
> ... The terrorists are asking the newspapers to publish their manifesto. All the newspapers have received a copy of it. So far as we know only one has published it: a newspaper whose speciality is popular news items preferably with something bloody on the front page, and whose journalists are not syndicated. You can guess what "liberty of the press" would mean under the rule of the FLQ: publish or don't publish this or that or else I kill ...
>
> ... The main thing is to keep calm. Nobody can win over people who aren't so inclined. The terrorists' strength depends on an understanding with the people. There is no such understanding here. There will be more acts of terrorism, but it doesn't take root amongst our people. It is still a marginal phenomenon.

Surprisingly, the English-Canadian press initially revealed considerable moderation, and even insight. Most editorial writers attempted to distinguish between the democratic separatism of the Parti québécois and the terrorism of the FLQ, although most continued to see the FLQ as more nationalist than radical. The *Toronto Star* (October 6) was almost alone in urging the government to meet the FLQ demands, "after bargaining for a reduced ransom" as if the critical issue were gold ingots. With Mr Cross safe, however, "there should be an end to any notion of truce or tolerance for the FLQ. The time is overdue for a massive police drive by both federal and provincial authorities to smash this pestilent organization once and for all. And if special criminal legislation is needed to secure this result, Parliament should give it early consideration at the present session." Most editorial writers and columnists did not advocate accepting the

FLQ demands, but (like the Toronto *Telegram*, October 7) hoped that there was some middle ground between that and the death of Mr Cross. The *Montreal Star* (October 7) vehemently objected to the words "political prisoners" used by the FLQ and repeated by men such as Robert Lemieux, and argued that "there could be no yielding to the kind of extortion which would threaten the most basic principles of democratic rule." The *Star*'s experienced columnist, W. A. Wilson, wrote a day later that the ultimatum had to be rejected as clearly as the submarine captain had to seal the doors of a leaking hull. The *Winnipeg Free Press* (October 8) bluntly asserted that the FLQ was guilty of treason – or should be – and that death remained the penalty for treason.

Writing in *Le Journal de Montréal* (October 8) René Lévesque again dissociated the Parti québécois from the FLQ and repudiated the "sewer rats" who resorted to kidnapping. But "the blind brutality of bureaucracies, technologies, and so-called 'growth' economies appear more important than human beings," he added, and "the all too frequent and visible collusion between private exploitation and public administration"

Chronicle-Herald, Halifax, October 7, 1970

were an understandable basis for terrorism and revolution. Michel Chartrand of the Montreal CNTU went further: "I have no more sympathy for Mrs Cross than for the wives of thousands of men without jobs in Quebec at the present time"; while Paul Cliche, leader of the Front d'action politique (FRAP), which was contesting the Montreal civic election, declared that those who loudly condemned terrorism were "pharisees" and that "the violence of a system which has produced so many unemployed is much worse and much more to be condemned." FRAP did not endorse the violence of the FLQ and had chosen "to play honestly the democratic game," added Mr Cliche. "But neither will FRAP condemn the two or three contestants who loose their head. When an unfortunate incident happens, everyone gets nervous, makes proclamations, and throws their hands up in despair. It is a pharisaism."

By October 8 police had rounded up a number of suspects, and were frequently rumoured to be within hours of locating the kidnappers. Rumours from Montreal, well-founded as it happened, indicated that Mrs Cross and the maid had identified one of the kidnappers (who had forgotten to put on their hoods) as Jacques Lanctôt, but no publicity was given and no warrant issued.

At 2:30 on the afternoon of October 8 another tip to CKLM led to the fifth FLQ communiqué in a telephone booth on rue Jean Talon:

Communiqué no 5, October 8, 1970, 12 o'clock (noon) delay 12 hours.

The Front de libération du Québec is warning the ruling authorities one last time. If by twelve midnight the authorities have not:

1 Proven their good faith in broadcasting our political manifesto on the airwaves of Radio-Canada as stipulated in Communiqué no 4;

2 Ordered fascist police forces to stop immediately their raids, persecutions, arrests, or tortures;

The Front de libération du Québec will be obliged to do away with diplomat J. Cross.

Once these conditions are met, the FLQ asks the authorities to specify exactly what they describe as irrational demands.

As for guarantees that the ruling authorities want specified, they must rest on the good faith of the two parties involved. We repeat, we are not putting the life of J. Cross at stake for a question of dollars.

We will release diplomat Cross within twenty-four hours following the realization of another condition dealing with the liberation of "consenting" political prisoners.

We shall overcome.

Front de libération du Québec.

Note: We reject the idea of a mediator; we will continue to establish our communications in our own way, avoiding the traps set by the fascist police.

By six o'clock Robert Lemieux had found television cameras to provide his view of the deepening crisis. The federal government, he said, almost as if speaking directly to the FLQ, "claims it wants to negotiate ... but all this is another way to try to fool the FLQ, while gaining as much time as possible so the police can find where the kidnappers are holding Cross and so they can start a gunfight and cause an execution."

The FLQ Manifesto

Whether the cell chose to believe Mr Lemieux or not, the government accepted one demand and instructed Radio-Canada to broadcast the FLQ manifesto. For thirteen minutes Gaston Montreuil sat before the cameras to read in a monotone the following document:

The Front de libération du Québec is not a messiah, nor a modern-day Robin Hood. It is a group of Quebec workers who have decided to use every means to make sure that the people of Quebec take control of their destiny.

The Front de libération du Québec wants the total independence of all Québécois, united in a free society, purged forever of the clique of voracious sharks, the patronizing "big bosses" and their henchmen who have made Quebec their hunting preserve for "cheap labour" and unscrupulous exploitation.

The Front de libération du Québec is not a movement of aggression, but is a response to the aggression organized by high finance and the puppet governments in Ottawa and Quebec (the Brinks "show," Bill 63, the electoral map, the so-called social progress tax, Power Corporation, "Doctors' insurance," the Lapalme guys ...)

The Front de libération du Québec finances itself by "voluntary taxes" taken from the same enterprises that exploit the workers (banks, finance companies, etc. ...)

"The money power of the status quo, the majority of the traditional teachers of our people, have obtained the reaction they hoped for; a backward step rather than the change for which we have worked as never before, for which we will continue to work" (René Lévesque, April 29, 1970).

We believed once that perhaps it would be worth it to channel our energy and our impatience, as Réne Lévesque said so well, into the Parti québécois, but the Liberal victory clearly demonstrated that that which we call democracy in Quebec is nothing but the democracy of the rich. The Liberal party's victory was nothing but the victory of the election riggers, Simard-Cotroni. As a result, the British parliamentary system is finished and the Front de libération du Québec will never allow itself to be fooled by the pseudo-elections that the Anglo-Saxon capitalists toss to the people of Quebec every four years. A number of Québécois have understood and will act. In the coming year Bourassa will have to face reality; 100,000 revolutionary workers, armed and organized.

Yes, there are reasons for the Liberal victory. Yes, there are reasons for poverty, unemployment, slums, and for the fact that you, Mr Bergeron of Visitation Street and you, Mr Legendre of Laval who earn $10,000 a year, will not feel free in our country of Quebec.

QUÉBEC-PRESSE

MAGAZINE SEMAINE DU 14 JUIN 1970. VOL. 2 NO 24

Les vrais "boss" du Québec

pages 2a et 3a

Québec-Presse, June 14, 1970

Yes, there are reasons, and the guys at Lord know them, the fishermen of the Gaspé, the workers of the North Shore, the miners for the Iron Ore Company, Quebec Cartier Mining, and Noranda, also know these reasons. And the brave workers of Cabano that you tried to screw again know lots of reasons.

Yes, there are reasons why you, Mr Tremblay of Panet Street and you Mr Cloutier, who work in construction in St Jérôme, cannot pay for "Vaisseaux d'or" with all the jazz and oom-pa-pa like Drapeau the aristocrat, who is so concerned with slums that he puts coloured billboards in front of them to hide our misery from the tourists.

Yes, there are reasons why you, Mrs Lemay of St Hyacinthe, can't pay for little trips to Florida like our dirty judges and parliamentary members do with our money.

The brave workers for Vickers and Davie Ship, who were thrown out and not given a reason, know these reasons. And the Murdochville men, who were attacked for the simple and sole reason that they wanted to organize a union and who were forced to pay $2 million by the dirty judges simply because they tried to exercise this basic right – they know justice and they know the reasons.

Yes, there are reasons why you, Mr Lachance of St Marguerite Street, must go and drown your sorrows in a bottle of that dog's beer, Molson. And you, Lachance's son, with your marijuana cigarettes ...

Yes, there are reasons why you, the welfare recipients, are kept from generation to generation on social welfare. Yes, there are all sorts of reasons, and the Domtar workers in East Angus and Windsor know them well. And the workers at Squibb and Ayers, and the men at the Liquor Board and those at Seven-Up and Victoria Precision, and the blue collar workers in Laval and Montreal and the Lapalme boys know those reasons well.

The Dupont of Canada workers know them as well, even if soon they will only be able to express them in English (thus assimilated they will enlarge the number of immigrants and New Quebeckers, the darlings of Bill 63).

And the Montreal policemen, those strongarms of the system, should understand these reasons – they should have been able to see we live in a terrorized society because, without their force, without their violence, nothing could work on October 7.

We have had our fill of Canadian federalism which penalizes the Quebec milk producers to satisfy the needs of the Anglo-Saxons of the Commonwealth; the system which keeps the gallant Montreal taxi drivers in a state of semi-slavery to shamefully protect the exclusive monopoly of the nauseating Murray Hill and its proprietor – the murderer Charles Hershorn and his son Paul, who, on the night of October 7, repeatedly grabbed the twelve-gauge shot gun from his employees hands to fire upon the taxi drivers and thereby mortally wound corporal Dumas, killed while demonstrating.

We have had our fill of a federal system which exercises a policy of heavy importation while turning out into the street the low wage-earners in the textile and shoe manufacturing trades, who are the most ill-treated in Quebec, for the benefit of a clutch of damned money-makers in their Cadillacs who rate the Quebec nation on the same level as other ethnic minorities in Canada.

We have had our fill, as have more and more Québécois, of a government

Québec-Presse, May 31, 1970

which performs a-thousand-and-one acrobatics to charm American millionaires into investing in Quebec, La Belle Province, where thousands and thousands of square miles of forests, full of game and well-stocked lakes, are the exclusive preserve of the almighty twentieth century lords.

We have had our fill of a hypocrite like Bourassa who relies on Brinks armoured trucks, the living symbol of the foreign occupation of Quebec, to keep the poor natives of Quebec in the fear of misery and unemployment in which they are accustomed to living.

We have had our fill of taxes which the Ottawa representative to Quebec wants to give to the Anglophone bosses to encourage them to speak French, old boy, to negotiate in French: Repeat after me: "Cheap labour means manpower in a healthy market."

We have had our fill of promises of jobs and prosperity while we always remain the cowering servants and boot-lickers of the big shots who live in Westmount, Town of Mount Royal, Hampstead, and Outremont; all the fortresses of high finance on St James and Wall streets, while we, the Québécois, have not used all our means, including arms and dynamite, to rid ourselves of these economic and political bosses who are prepared to use every sort of sordid tactic to better screw us.

We live in a society of terrorized slaves, terrorized by the big bosses like Steinberg, Clark, Bronfman, Smith, Neaple, Timmins, Geoffrion, J. L. Lévesque, Hershorn, Thompson, Nesbitt, Desmarais, Kierans. Compared to them Rémi Popol the lousy no-good, Drapeau the Dog, Bourassa the lackey of the Simards, and Trudeau the fairy are peanuts.

We are terrorized by the capitalist Roman church, even though this seems less and less obvious (who owns the property on which the stock exchange stands?); by the payments to pay back Household Finance; by the publicity of the overlords of retail trade like Eaton, Simpson, Morgan, Steinberg, and General Motors; we are terrorized by the closed circles of science and culture which are the universities and by their bosses like Gaudry and Dorais and by the underling Robert Shaw.

The number of those who realize the oppression of this terrorist society are growing and the day will come when all the Westmounts of Quebec will disappear from the map.

Production workers, miners, foresters, teachers, students, and unemployed workers, take what belong to you, your jobs, your right to decide, and your liberty. And you, workers of General Electric, it's you who makes your factories run, only you are capable of production; without you General Electric is nothing!

Workers of Quebec, start today to take back what is yours; take for yourselves what belongs to you. Only you know your factories, your machines, your hotels, your universities, your unions. Don't wait for an organizational miracle.

Make your own revolution in your areas, in your places of work. And if you don't do it yourselves, other usurpers, technocrats and so on will replace the handful of cigar smokers we now know, and everything will be the same again. Only you are able to build a free society.

We must fight, not singly, but together. We must fight until victory is ours with all the means at our disposal as did the patriots of 1837–38 (those whom our sacred Mother church excommunicated to sell out to the British interests).

In the four corners of Quebec, may those who have been contemptuously called lousy French and alcoholics start fighting their best against the enemies of liberty and justice and prevent all the professional swindlers and robbers, the bankers, the businessmen, the judges, and the sold-out politicators from causing harm.

We are the workers of Quebec and we will continue to the bitter end. We want to replace the slave society with a free society, functioning by itself and for itself; a society open to the world.

Our struggle can only lead to victory. You cannot hold an awakening people in misery and contempt indefinitely. Long live Free Quebec!

Long live our imprisoned political comrades.

Long live the Quebec revolution!

Long live the Front de libération du Québec.

For the first time many English Canadians, and perhaps many Québécois as well, realized that the FLQ were something other than separatists in a hurry.

Early on the morning of October 9 the FLQ responded to the broadcast with Communiqué no 6, setting more limited conditions for the release of Mr Cross. The message was either not found or not released. That afternoon at three Mr Choquette released a brief message to the kidnappers asking for proof that Cross was still alive in the form of a handwritten note containing the sentence: "It is now five days since I left and I want you to know, darling, that I miss you every minute." The FLQ replied at six with Communiqué no 7, and included a copy of no 6:

Communiqué no 6,October 8 [*sic*], 8 o'clock AM.

The Front de libération du Québec suspends temporarily its threat to execute the diplomat J. Cross, following the broadcast of the political manifesto by Radio-Canada.

Here are the two final conditions which the ruling authorities must meet to keep diplomat J. Cross alive:

First: liberation of "consenting" political prisoners and their transportation to Cuba or Algeria, as set out in the first communiqué, items 3 and 4.

The wives and children of the political prisoners must be allowed to accompany them if they so desire.

Lawyer Robert Lemieux, Pierre Pascau, and Louis Fournier must be allowed to witness these operations and see to it that they are carried out satisfactorily.

Second: the immediate suspension of all searches, raids, arrests, and tortures on the part of the fascist police forces.

When we decided to abduct the diplomat Cross, we took into consideration all possibilities, including that of the sacrifice of our lives for a cause that we believe to be right. If the police forces ever happened to discover us and tried to intervene before the release of British diplomat Cross, be sure that we will defend our lives dearly and that J. Cross would be executed at once. And we have enough dynamite to feel "safe."

Guarantee:

The Front de libération du Québec pledges solemnly before the Quebec people to release diplomat J. Cross alive and well within the twenty-four hours following the return to Montreal of the observers who accompany the political prisoners.

Upon their return these observers must confirm publicly that the operations were completed satisfactorily.

We shall overcome

Front de libération du Québec.

Note: enclosed is a public letter by J. Cross. This letter was hand written by Mr Cross at three o'clock this afternoon.

Communiqué no 7, October 8 [*sic*], 1970, 6 o'clock PM, time limit: 24 hours.

The Front de libération du Québec forwarded Communiqué no 6 to the ruling authorities via Mr Trudel of the newspaper *La Semaine*. That envelope was addressed to Pierre Pascau and was deposited at 4055 St Joseph, under the carpet of the entrance hallway.

We are now certain that the ruling authorities are only trying to gain time since they refuse to tell the population about the contents of Communiqué no 6 as well as a public letter from J. Cross.

This is the last communiqué in the event that the ruling authorities do not free the political prisoners between now and six o'clock, Saturday night. Neither the ruling authorities nor their fascist political police will find the diplomat J. Cross if they do not carry out our demands as set out in Communiqué no 6 within the above-mentioned time limit.

We shall overcome.

Front de libération du Québec.

Note no 1: we are attaching a letter from J. Cross repeating the phrase asked for by the dog Choquette.

Note no 2: we are also attaching a copy of communiqué no 6.

[A handwritten note – partly in long hand and partly in block letters – noted:]

It is imperative that our communiqué be broadcast by a radio station (CKLM or CKAC).

Do your utmost and give it by hand to a reporter.

Thank you.

As Saturday dawned Robert Lemieux held a press conference solemnly to assure anyone listening that James Cross, with his M-15 counter-espionage experience, was using his letters to reveal his whereabouts. At 3 PM he found the press again to declare that he would regard it as an honour to accompany the kidnappers to Cuba or Algeria, and to announce that a group called the Vigilantes had warned him that he and his family would be killed if Cross were executed. During the day there were undoubtedly conversations between Ottawa and Quebec, and a decision seems either to have been reached or confirmed that negotiations between the governments and the FLQ should be handled from Quebec. The *Toronto Star*'s Ottawa bureau filed this story on October 12:

> Why was a Quebec cabinet minister charged with the duty of giving Canada's answer to the diplomat's kidnappers?
>
> Sharp revealed the official reasons to The Star in an interview last night, and other federal government sources filled in the background details of the decision.
>
> Officials said federal and provincial government strategists bargaining to save the diplomat's life had to consider, among other things, the political climate of Quebec and the apparent attitude of the province's people to the kidnapping.
>
> They concluded that the overwhelming majority of Quebeckers were horrified.
>
> They believed, also, the sources said, that the people of Quebec at large would be sympathetic to any stated declaration that the province's government would seek to reform its institutions by democratic processes, and not under the threat of violence.
>
> But that message, because of Canada's delicate federal nature, could be delivered only by a Quebecker – and a member of the Quebec government.

Whatever the explanation, a half an hour before the 6 PM deadline – a deadline most people took more seriously than the others – Mr Choquette read a prepared statement on television:

> The feeling within the person speaking is one of social reconciliation, of acceptance of change, of the abolition of ambiguity and distrust, and of the rallying of all Québécois, despite our differences of opinion, around a common ideal. The problem is raised dramatically by the abduction of Mr Cross, but it involves us all. No society can expect that the decisions of its governments, or of its courts of law, can be questioned or overthrown by resorting to blackmail on the part of a group; for this implies an end to all social order, and represents a denial of the freedom of individuals and groups for this freedom can only express itself within the institutional framework which resolves the conflicts and the interests of groups involved.
>
> I understand that it is by virtue of a particular conception of society that the authors of the abduction of Mr Cross have acted. But this conception they cannot impose upon the majority of their fellow citizens by violence or by murder, which would in effect discredit it forever. Without giving in to undue pressure, even dangerous pressure, the "ruling authorities," as you say, are not unaware that there are areas of discontent within our society and that injustice exists.
>
> I think that Mr Cross' kidnappers are mature and adult enough to admit, first of all, that in this field there is need for difference of opinion. They are completely free to predicate their opinions in speeches and in action so long as they do not resort to violence or to murder of an innocent person. On the contrary, these opinions can be expressed in a chat or a frank, open discussion between the different elements of society, so as to contribute to a constructive and positive solution of our problems.

The government of Quebec is a government dedicated to reform. It is deeply concerned with social justice for all its citizens, especially the most needy.

Therefore, the proposal which I can put forward at the present time is to ask you to take account of our good faith, and of our desire to examine objectively the injustices of our society.

What mechanism, what institution, should we set up?

The government is making a serious effort to listen to all social groups. The respect and interest shown in citizens' committees is a proof of our concern for the reform of our society.

In conjunction with all those who are aware of such reforms as are needed we intend to examine improvements to our structures so that the demands of citizens and of groups may be heard and so that the state's action may comply with social evolution.

It would be a denial of these efforts to take measures which would end in the destruction of the social order that we are building. This is why we cannot remain silent on the subject of the so-called political prisoners. A parole procedure is in force which applies to all prisoners, which will be carried out objectively. This also means that the cases which are presently before the courts in connection with some of the accused must be judged, otherwise this would yet again be the destruction of the social order which we must build. But we will consider the cases with clemency, with a clemency that is opportune in view of your gesture which should put an end to terrorism here.

As a final concession to save the life of Mr Cross, the federal government has instructed me that it is prepared to offer you safe conduct to a foreign country. If, on the other hand, you choose to refuse such safe conduct, I can assure you that you will be granted all possible clemency before our courts in view of any humanitarian gesture you make to spare the life of Mr Cross. This I can promise you.

I therefore ask you as a gesture of absolute good faith: release Mr Cross immediately.

Rising above all individual considerations, we must build a society which deals effectively with justice and liberty. Gentlemen: you have your part to play in this matter if you so choose.

A Second Hostage–Pierre Laporte

OCTOBER 10–14

AS Jérôme Choquette spoke four men leaped into a 1968 Chevrolet. Half an hour later Pierre Laporte, forty-nine-year-old minister of labour and of immigration in the Bourassa cabinet, was the captive of the FLQ's Chenier cell. The story of the kidnapping was allegedly told by Paul Rose, one of the kidnappers, after his capture:

I, Paul Rose, born October 16, 1943, of 5630 Armstrong Street, St Hubert, do solemnly declare that I am also known by the names of Paul Blais and Paul Fournier. I rented the house at 5630 Armstrong Street in St Hubert in company with Lise Balcer about March 1970. I introduced Lise as my wife, Lise Blais, since I went under the name of Paul Blais at that time.

Lise Balcer lived with us there until July 1970. Francis Simard, Bernard Lortie, and Jacques Rose also lived there. During that period, we were visited by Jacques Cossette-Trudel and his wife; and also, in August or early September 1970, Jacques Lanctôt, his wife Suzanne Lanctôt, and their son, Boris, lived with us at 5630 Armstrong Street in St Hubert for a couple of weeks.

Jean-Luc Arène, Normand Turgeon, and Marc Carbonneau also came to the house. About the end of August or early September the group split up and it was then that the Liberation cell and the Chenier financial cell were formed.

The Liberation cell was comprised of Marc Carbonneau, Yves Langlois, Jacques and Louise Cossette-Trudel, and Jacques Lanctôt. This cell was to carry out two kidnappings simultaneously, involving James Cross and an American named James Le Cou.

As for the Chenier financial cell, it comprised Paul Rose, Jacques Rose, and Francis Simard; Bernard Lortie was considered as a stand-by. We were supposed to look after the financing of the movement, which consisted of two cells.

About September 23 or 24, 1970, Jacques Rose, Francis Simard and I left with my mother and my sister, Claire Rose, in the yellow 1969 Plymouth Valiant automobile belonging to my mother. We were planning to raise funds for the FLQ (Front de libération du Québec) movement.

While we were in Texas, in Dallas, we were trying to buy firearms, revolvers, and we even paid one individual $30 to make the purchase. We heard on the radio about the kidnapping of James Richard Cross. When we learned that there was only one hostage, we decided we had to return to Canada, in case the government refused to meet the demands of the Liberation cell. And so we arrived in Longueuil on Thursday morning, October 8, 1970.

We dropped my mother and Claire Rose off at the Towers shopping centre in Greenfield Park. Jacques Rose, Francis Simard, and I went to a motel, the name of which I don't know, on Taschereau Boulevard, not far from the Claude St Jean Restaurant.

We stayed there for a day to give Francis time to spend a day on Armstrong Street in St Hubert so that we could find out whether the house had been spotted and put under watch.

Since the house was not being watched, we went there the next morning, Friday, October 9. That day, Francis Simard, Jacques Rose, and I talked about the attitude of the government regarding the Cross case. We also discussed and prepared the kidnapping of Pierre Laporte.

We knew where he lived and we went there to watch his comings and goings. We came to Montreal by bus to buy wigs and disguises.

Then we went back to the house and we discussed the strategy we should use to pull off the abduction of Laporte. Since we had to be four men to execute the plan, Jacques contacted a person whom I will call x.

This person came to join us that same night at 5630 Armstrong Street in St Hubert, and spent the night with us at 5630 Armstrong.

On Saturday, October 10, 1970, the four of us got up and agreed on our strategy. Then we tried out our disguises. It was agreed at that time that we would use the blue Chevrolet with the black vinyl top. It was a 1968 model Chevrolet Biscayne bearing 1970 Quebec licence plate number 9J–2420.

The car was registered in the name of Paul Fournier and the papers had been signed by Pierre Séguin, alias Yves Langlois.

That afternoon, Jacques Rose and Francis Simard went for a drive to reconnoitre the area around the Laporte residence. Jacques Rose drove the dark blue 1968 Chevrolet with the dark vinyl top and the 1970 Quebec licence plates 9J–2420.

When they came back, we listened to the news and while Justice Minister Jérôme Choquette was replying to the Liberation cell, we decided to leave. Jacques Rose got into the driver's seat of the blue 1968 Chevrolet and Mr x sat in front on the right. I sat in the back on the right and Francis Simard was to my left.

We had prepared our wigs and disguises during the afternoon. We drove from 5630 Armstrong, St Hubert, on to La Savane Road, then on a sideroad to Highway 20, on to Highway 3, and into Longueuil. Then we drove along Riverside, to Tiffin Road and Robitaille.

When we saw there was some activity at the home of Pierre Laporte and that his car was in the driveway, we decided to make a telephone call to make sure he was really there.

Jacques called from a phone booth in front of a restaurant opposite the Tropicana in Longueuil. A female voice replied that Pierre Laporte was about to leave home.

We drove along Tiffin and another street crossing Robillard. While driving on this street, we could watch both the house and the car belonging to Laporte.

Finally, one of us saw Laporte playing football in a field opposite his home. The one who saw him told us and, at that instant, we turned the corner and headed on Robillard towards the place where Laporte was.

As we turned the corner, Mr X put on his hood, which was made with a green army-style cap with two eye slits cut out of the ear flap. Francis Simard and I each carried an M-1 automatic rifle and Mr X had a sawn-off shotgun.

So we drove towards the spot where Laporte was. It was about 6 PM.

When we got near Laporte, Jacques Rose braked abruptly and the tires squealed. As soon as we stopped, I got out with Mr X. I walked up to Pierre Laporte with my gun loaded and aimed at him, and I ordered him to get into the car.

I told him, "Get into the car and be quick about it."

Laporte was stupefied and he did not move. Mr X then grabbed him by the arm and led him to the car.

Meanwhile, Jacques Rose stayed at the wheel and Francis Simard remained seated in the back of the car, pointing his gun at Laporte.

When Laporte got into the car, he sat down in the middle of the rear seat and the car moved off almost instantly. I told him how to lie down on the floor of the car between the two seats and he did, and Francis and I had to throw our weight against the seat. I also told him to close his eyes so he would not see us.

Laporte complied with all our demands and he was quite calm throughout the trip.

We drove down Robillard Street, Logan Street, Tiffin Road, and St Paul Street. At the corner of St Paul and Taschereau Boulevard, Francis Simard got off with a communiqué that he had to deliver to a radio station.

This communiqué had been prepared in advance by the four members of the Chenier cell.

Jacques, Mr X, and I then drove along Taschereau Boulevard with Laporte on to Laurier and the St Hubert traffic circle.

While going over the railway tracks we crossed a patrol car from the St Hubert police and its red dome light began flashing. I told Jacques and X to look straight ahead to avoid attracting attention and I made this comment: "They must have just heard the bulletin."

After that, we drove to 5630 Armstrong via La Savane, passing in front of the St Hubert air base. When we reached the house, Mr X opened the garage door and we drove in quickly.

After closing the door, we led Laporte into the house proper through an opening in the wall we had made a month or two previously.

We had made this opening because, when we arrived at the house and we were more than two in the car, those in the back seat had to hide by lying down on the seat. And we entered the same way as when we arrived with Laporte.

This was to hide from the neighbours how many persons came to our house.

Before Laporte entered the house, I asked him to sit up in the rear seat of the car and to shut his eyes. When he did this, Jacques and I blindfolded him with green adhesive tape. Then we guided him into the house and into a bedroom in the right rear corner of the house. Once he was in this room, someone handcuffed him and tied his handcuffs to the bed on which he lay. After he was installed there, Jacques, X, and I organized a watch with one man in front and one in back for eight-hour shifts.

A New Sense of Urgency

The nation was stunned as it appeared that the FLQ could kidnap at will. The police accelerated their activity. Prime Minister Bourassa moved into heavily guarded quarters in the Queen Elizabeth Hotel. And, in what was described as routine military operations, troops of the Royal 22nd moved towards Montreal. Messages were apparently sent to prominent Québécois warning them that the government could not be responsible for their safety. Early on Sunday morning police arrested Robert Lemieux, who the previous evening had described the kidnappings of Cross and Laporte as the logical end of the struggle begun by the FLQ in 1964, on the following warrant:

On or about October 9, 1970, Robert Lemieux did wilfully and illegally impede police agents in the execution of their duty during the course of an inquiry relating to the abduction of the commercial attaché James Richard Cross on October 5, 1970, by making declarations which delayed or complicated their task, thereby committing a criminal act in accordance with article 110-A of the penal code.

Earlier that morning reporter Daniel McGinnis of CKAC had been informed of an envelope near the Peel subway station. Located at 9 AM, it contained the first communiqué from the Chenier cell:

In the face of the persistence of the governmental authorities in not complying with the requirements of the FLQ and in conformity with Plan 3 established earlier to provide for such a refusal, the Chenier financial cell has just kidnapped the Minister of Unemployment and Quebec Assimilation, Pierre Laporte.

The minister will be executed Sunday evening at 10 PM if between now and then the ruling authorities have not responded favourably to the seven demands set forth following the kidnapping of Mr James Cross. Any partial acceptance will be considered as a refusal.

In the meantime, the Liberation cell will make known the technical details of the whole operation.

We shall overcome.

Front de libération du Québec.

At one o'clock CKAC was informed of another communication, containing a letter from Pierre Laporte to his wife:

FLQ
Chenier Financial Cell
Communiqué no 2 (last)

This is the last communication between the Chenier financial cell and the

Québec-Presse, September 27, 1970

ruling authorities. The Liberation cell, that is to say the one which carried out the kidnapping of James Cross, is to send you a communiqué setting forth the general situation.

We repeat that if between now and 10 PM this evening the two governments have not responded favourably to the seven conditions of the FLQ, the minister Pierre Laporte will be executed. Pierre Laporte will be released within twenty-four hours of the complete realization, that is to say, of the seven conditions of Operation Liberation.

The least hesitation by the ruling authorities will be fatal for the minister. It is already a very great concession for us to undertake to return him alive and in good condition. You must not ask too much of us.

We shall overcome.

Front de libération du Québec.

P.S.: the first communiqué was sent to radio station CKAC at 9 AM.

October 12 [*sic*], 1970, 7 AM.

Darling,

I am well, in good health, and I have spent a good night.

I insist that you and the children accept things in such a way as not to affect your health.

I am constantly thinking of you and this helps me to stand up to things.

The main thing is that the authorities take action.

My love to everyone.

Pierre.

That afternoon, while wild rumours filled the air waves and Bourassa met with his ministers, the FLQ drafted a third communiqué, which they sent to CKAC at 4:45 along with a letter from Laporte to Bourassa:

Due to technical circumstances beyond our control, we had to prepare the second communiqué in handwriting. This document is intended, then, to confirm the authenticity of Communiqué no 2.

This communication between the Chenier cell and the ruling authorities is the last one. Either the government accepts it or does not. Gone are the acts of favour, maybes, and promises. We know what we want, where we are going, and we are determined to get there.

We have had no news from the Liberation cell. Normally, if Mr James Cross is still alive, the members of the cell should send out an eighth communiqué. If Mr Cross has not been executed, the communiqué will sum up the situation. If Mr Cross has been executed then we will continue Operation Liberation. We will then issue another communiqué when the governments have made their decision or their indecision known, as the case may be. The last communiqué will deal with the freeing or execution of Pierre Laporte. Finally, if Mr Cross is still alive and for reasons beyond their control the Liberation cell is not able to put out an eighth communiqué the diplomat will be freed at the same time as Pierre Laporte.

We shall overcome.

Front de libération du Québec.

Sunday 3 PM.
Mr Robert Bourassa
My dear Robert:

1 I feel I am writing the most important letter of my life.

2 At the moment I am in perfect health. I am well treated, even with courtesy.

3 I insist that police stop all their searches to find me. If they succeeded this would result in a murderous shoot-out from which I shall certainly not come out alive.

4 In other words, you have the power to dispose of my life. If this were the only question and if this sacrifice were to produce good results, one could entertain it, but we are facing a well-organized escalation which will only end with the release of the "political prisoners." After me, there will be a third one, then a fourth, and a twentieth. If all political men are protected, they will strike elsewhere, in other classes of society. One might as well act now and avoid a bloodbath and an altogether unnecessary panic.

5 You know my own case, which should be borne in mind. I had two brothers. They are dead, both of them. I remain alone as head of a large family which includes my mother, my sister, my own wife, and my children as well as the children of Roland, whose guardian I am. My departure would mean an irreparable loss. For you know the closeness which unites the members of my family. I am no longer the only one whose fate is at stake, but a dozen people are involved – all women and young children. I think that you understand!

6 If the departure of the "political prisoners" is organized and carried out satisfactorily, I am certain that my personal security as well as that of those who would follow will be absolute.

This could be done rapidly, as I cannot see why, in taking more time, they should continue to make me die little by little where I am presently detained. Decide ... on my life or on my death. I rely on you and thank you.

Friendly greetings,
Pierre Laporte.

P.S. I repeat: have the searches stopped and don't let the police carry them on without your knowledge. The success of such a search would mean a death warrant for me.

Although a poll by Information Collection Institute (published on October 19) revealed that 78 per cent of Montrealers totally disapproved of the kidnappings, while only one per cent totally approved, and a majority believed that "the maintenance of law and order" was more important than saving two lives, it was clear that articulate Quebec, at least, was by no means unanimous. Journalists declared categorically that the Bourassa cabinet was deeply split following the Laporte kidnapping. The editors of *Québec-Presse* (October 11), the left-wing newspaper financed by the trade unions, were hardly severe in their editorial "Le FLQ et nous":

To our way of thinking the shattering diagnosis attributed to the sickness in

Quebec by the Front de libération du Québec (FLQ) is well-founded and correct.

It is true that "the Brink's show, Bill 63, the electoral map, the so-called 'social progress' tax, the Power Corporation, medical insurance, the Lapalme guys ..." (mentioned in the FLQ manifesto) are all signs of the innate corruption within our political and economic system. Only those who are blinded by self-interest or by lack of awareness could fail to admit as much.

This corruption brings about slavery amongst vast areas of the population and turns into aggression. This aggression is violent: slums, lack of medical treatment, union members attacked by armed police, jail sentences (for example, Murdochville), and special legislation. In answer to this violence the FLQ intends to respond with violence. A type of violence aimed at getting rid of the oppressors to replace them with a political and economic system based on the needs of the people of Quebec and controlled by them. This new society will be open to the world and will be founded on respect for the rights of people and races.

The greatest danger represented by terrorist action is its secrecy. Its power to work underground. Its armed strength. And yet the oppressor also – particularly in the case of Quebec and under a front of legality – acts in secrecy: the real transactions, in big financial circles, take place in secrecy. Similarly for electoral funds. The real power over life and death, sometimes physical power over citizens, which is in the hands of the "heavyweights" of our system, also remains hidden. What goes on between the large corporations and governments is not revealed. Only what can't be camouflaged is revealed. The oppressor is armed too.

Clandestine action is chosen for tactical reasons: when and in what circumstances is terrorist action justified? This much is certain, it is not up to those in power to pass judgment. The winners of the last election – whose victory is only due to a minority, and which sprang from a libellous and racist electoral campaign with the added insurance of the Brinks-Royal Trust trucks – are not in a position to teach anyone any moral, political, or social lessons.

The fact that the spokesmen of an establishment which has been denounced by the FLQ take it upon themselves to speak on behalf of the majority and to condemn terrorist action this week proves nothing – somebody whose action is disputed doesn't usually agree with his critic.

The only valid judgment possible can come from the people. In one week the FLQ has succeeded in talking to the people as never before. The FLQ's action has been a little like a course in political instruction by total immersion. A kind of political Berlitz. So the FLQ has achieved one main aim: namely, to speak in its own words to the world. And to keep the minds of the people of Quebec on their own situation.

As far as we are concerned – agreeing as we do with the FLQ's aims without approving the methods – we reckon that the struggle for the liberation of Quebec is a basic requirement. This aim is incorporated in *Québec-Presse*'s declaration of principles.

Our part in this struggle is to try to keep it going in the press.

Editorial Committee

The permanent council of FRAP (Front d'action politique, an organization of trade unions, local committee groups, students, and intellectuals then contesting the civic election in Montreal) met the same day, with most of the candidates absent and endorsed the objectives of the FLQ manifesto. Although FRAP itself chose to work through democratic means, it observed that the terrorism of the FLQ was directed not against the workers but against the violence of the establishment. As Bourassa met with his cabinet at the Queen Elizabeth on Sunday afternoon, Claude Ryan met his staff in the less luxurious editorial offices of *Le Devoir*. Ryan clearly had little confidence in the strength of the Bourassa government – at least to pursue the line he favoured – and had apparently urged Mr Bourassa early Sunday morning to think of reinforcing his government with people from the opposition or outside active politics. As he explained it later (*Le Devoir*, October 30):

During telephone conversations with Messrs Lucien Saulnier and Robert Bourassa in the dark hours which followed the kidnapping of Pierre Laporte, I became aware of the dire confusion felt by the political authorities in the face of the crisis opened up by this second FLQ abduction. As early as the afternoon of Sunday, October 11, I called a meeting at the *Devoir* offices of my principal colleagues for the purpose of a joint appraisal of the situation. During our discussion three main hypotheses were put forward:

1 The possibility that the Bourassa government, in keeping with the hard line described the day before by Mr Jérôme Choquette and succumbing to pressure from Ottawa and Montreal, might be tempted to request immediate declaration of the War Measures Act, thereby giving Ottawa the primary responsibility for solving a crisis which concerned the leader of the Quebec government;

2 The possibility that, in the case of further developments, the Bourassa government might at one stage or another be reduced to impotence and be unable to control the situation. In this case there would probably be only one short-term solution: the formation of a provisional government team composed of the best people from the various provincial parties, backed up by a few political personalities from various milieus;

3 The possibility that the Bourassa government, in choosing to seek a negotiated solution and thereby demonstrating its responsibility, might come out of the crisis united and with a greater degree of confidence. In this case, however, our view was still that Mr Bourassa should think about strengthening his team after the crisis was over.

Of these three possibilities the third was far and away the most reasonable and realistic. We nevertheless decided to give thought to all three while keeping a watch on developments. After this meeting it was decided I should seek the advice – from an entirely private and confidential angle – of a few people including Mr Lucien Saulnier as regards our findings. That same day, towards the evening, I visited Mr Saulnier.

During this conversation Mr Saulnier appeared to favour a solution calling for the immediate application of war measures; the only thing which seemed to be holding him back was the emotion aroused in him by Pierre Laporte's

La Presse, Montreal, November 19, 1970

letter which had been made public one hour previously. The second hypothesis he rejected as unthinkable on a short-term basis. At no time during our talk did I mention a plan for a provisional government in which I myself would have played any part. I was seeking Mr Saulnier's advice in my capacity as a newspaper editor who had been asked to take a stand on the events which had taken place. Because of the developments which followed that same evening there were no other meetings.

Negotiations

Just five minutes before the ten o'clock deadline Prime Minister Bourassa emerged from lengthy cabinet discussions and communications with Ottawa to read a short statement over radio and television:

Exceptional and unprecedented events in our province threaten the stability of our political institutions.

What is fundamentally unjust and extremely dangerous is that we live in a place where freedom of speech and action is among the greatest in the world. Even the parties contesting the political régime itself all have freedom to express themselves. In fact, this freedom of speech has often been used in recent years in systematically sowing hatred and lies ...

The government cannot, must not, and will not remain passive when the welfare of the individual is threatened at its very roots. I am too proud of being a Québécois not to tell you of all my determination and that of the government I lead to overcome this very grave crisis.

In this work of safeguarding the fundamental values of our civilization, I am convinced that I have the support of all elected representatives of the people. I ask the population to show calm and confidence in these difficult circumstances. Indeed, the worth of our people, their exceptional spirit for work, their respect for others, and their sense of freedom are the best guarantees for the victory of justice and peace.

This basic situation, which should reassure us, must not make us forget, however, the extremely pressing problems caused by the fact that the lives of two men are at stake.

One is a typical Quebec politician devoted to the progress of his community; the other, a distinguished diplomat, not involved in the tensions faced by our society.

In this matter, the Front de libération du Québec has issued a communiqué demanding the integral and total acceptance of their seven demands. But, the Labour Minister has addressed to me a letter in which he deals with two questions: the searches by police and the release of the political prisoners ...

We all want – is it necessary to say it? – Mr Laporte and Mr Cross to live. Fate, in a rare example of how cruel it can be, has decided to choose them to be the issue on which maintenance of public order depends.

It is because we particularly want Mr Laporte and Mr Cross to live that we decide – before discussing the demands that have been made – to set up mechanisms that would guarantee, as Mr Laporte says it will, that the release of the political prisoners will surely result in the safe release of the hostages.

That is a prerequisite that common sense forces us to require and it is for this reason that we ask the kidnappers to contact us.

Indeed, how can one accede to the demands without being convinced that the counterpart will be fulfilled? The Quebec government believes that it would be irresponsible towards the state and to Mr Laporte and Mr Cross if it did not insist on this safeguard.

We want to save the lives of Mr Laporte and Mr Cross and it is because we want it with all our strength that we are making this gesture.

My dear fellow citizens, a great statesman said once: "To govern is to choose." We have chosen justice – individual and collective.

As far as I am concerned I shall fight for such justice to the limits of my powers, assuming all risks whatever they are and as essential as they may be to the future of our people.

Within minutes of the end of his address, the Cross kidnappers drafted their reply which, along with a letter from Cross to Bourassa, they sent to CKLM where it was received at 1:45 on Monday morning, October 12:

Communiqué no 8, October 11, 1970, 10 PM.

Following the kidnapping of Pierre Laporte and the position adopted by the ruling authorities, the Front de libération du Québec repeats its last two demands contained in Communiqué no 6, to wit:

The release of "consenting" political prisoners and their safe conduct to either Cuba or Algeria, as stipulated in Communiqué no 1, items 3 and 4: wives and children should be allowed to accompany the prisoners if they so wish.

The political prisoners must be accompanied by their lawyer, Robert Lemieux, and reporters Pierre Pascau and Louis Fournier, to see and attend the carrying-out of the operation. Mr Lemieux should also serve as an intermediary between the two FLQ cells and the authorities.

An immediate halt to all searches, raids, and arrests by the fascist police forces.

Guarantees:

The Front de libération du Québec gives the people of Quebec its word of honour that it will release, safe and sound, both diplomat Cross and Laporte within twenty-four hours following the return to Montreal of the observers accompanying the imprisoned patriots.

Upon the return of observers to Montreal they should confirm that the operations went according to plan. For obvious reasons of security, we certainly cannot reveal where Mr Cross and Mr Laporte will be released, but the authorities will be informed of the place where Mr Cross and Mr Laporte can be found within minutes following this liberation.

We shall overcome.

Front de libération du Québec.

Note 1: We are not setting a time limit. We believe that the good faith of the authorities will be demonstrated by the speed with which they will fulfill these conditions. After all, our patience does have limits.

Note 2: We include with this communiqué a letter from J. Cross as proof that he is still alive.

October 11, 1970, 10 PM.
Dear Mr Bourassa,

I have just finished listening to your three-minute speech broadcast over Radio-Canada.

I am writing this note to assure you and the population of Quebec that I am alive and in good health.

As for the guarantees you request concerning my release in good health by the FLQ "Liberation cell," I can only say that personally I have complete confidence that they will keep their promise to release me in the twenty-four hours following the successful return to Quebec of the observers accompanying the consenting political prisoners and their wives and families.

You must understand that the FLQ cannot be more specific as to the modalities of my release without compromising their own security.

Tell my wife that I should be seeing her very soon.

Thank you for saving my life and that of Mr Laporte.

Your humanity in this difficult situation cannot help but be much appreciated by our families and friends.

Yours sincerely,
J. R. Cross.

The Chenier cell deliberated longer over the Bourassa speech, but by midnight had begun work on a response. When finished they included a letter from Laporte to Bourassa and informed CKAC, which located it at 10:50 AM, October 12:

Sunday, October 11, midnight.

Following the tacit acceptance of the demands of the Front by the government of Quebec here is the answer of the FLQ (Chenier cell):

1 We refuse to negotiate on the content of the six conditions which remain to be fulfilled.

2 As far as the technicalities of fulfilling the six conditions, we have full confidence in the revolutionary integrity of Robert Lemieux. We therefore appoint him intermediary for the Front. Each of his decisions will be final. He and we are as one.

3 The only guarantee that we can give as far as the freeing of Pierre Laporte is concerned is our word as Quebec revolutionaries. He will be released safe and sound in the twenty-four hours following the fulfilment of the FLQ demands.

4 As far as the freeing of Mr Cross is concerned, we can assure you that this will be done if he is still alive. However, since the Liberation cell has not given any sign of life, we cannot promise you anything about this ... We do not know if Mr Cross was executed or not. But we repeat that if James Cross is still alive he will be freed like Pierre Laporte.

5 As proof of our good faith we are suspending our activities and are asking the other cells to do the same.

6 Any hesitation by you will be considered as a tacit refusal and will lead to the execution of Pierre Laporte.

7 We are not setting any deadline; however, if you display an obvious lack of good faith we will take action.

We shall overcome.

Front de libération du Québec.

My dear Robert, I've just heard your speech. Thanks, I was expecting as much from you ... While eating very frugally this evening, I sometimes had the impression of having my last meal.

About the arrangements for the carrying-out of the conditions, they've told me you have already been informed. The ideal would be that the "political prisoners" leave as of Monday during the evening or during the night or Tuesday morning.

The remainder should be done at the same time. My friend the Honourable Jean-Pierre Côté must be told that the situation of the ex-Lapalme employees is primordial. Maybe we could place a certain number of them in CAT or at the minimum wage commission of Montreal or Quebec if they want to.

For the arrangements, discussions, and practical settlement, the people of the FLQ want lawyer Robert Lemieux. They are prepared to give him full authority ... from his prison if necessary. You may delegate who you want.

Would you be good enough on receiving this letter to telephone Françoise to reassure her and to give her and the children all kinds of good news from me.

You were asking, quite rightly, for guarantees about the freedom of Mr

Cross and myself. You were right. I am ready unconditionally to accept the word of my kidnappers and I ask of you to do the same.

Thanks again ... and thanks to all those who have contributed to this reasonable decision which you announced with strength and dignity.

I hope to be free ... and at work within twenty-four hours. With friendship, Pierre Laporte.

P.S. You can tell the handwriting specialist that this letter is indeed written by me. P.L.

Communication established by radio, the Chenier cell then undertook to summarize the situation on the afternoon of October 12. The communiqué was found at 4:30 and reached the public through Pierre Pascau of CKLM:

Following the publication of the eighth communiqué of the Liberation cell and the last communiqué from the Chenier finance cell, the situation is clearly established:

1 The safe and sound release of Mr Cross depends on acceptance of the following two stipulations: the liberation of the political prisoners, a halt to police repression.

2 The release of Pierre Laporte depends on the complete fulfilment of all six original conditions of the FLQ.

From this position, then, there are only three possible developments:

1 The government refuses all the demands, or hesitates to meet them, or takes too much time to answer. Faced with such a situation the two hostages will be executed.

2 The government decides to accept two conditions: liberation of the political prisoners, an end to police operations. In this case, James Cross will be freed during the twenty-four hours following the return of the three observers and the execution of Pierre Laporte will be lifted, unless the police forces discover the whereabouts of Pierre Laporte. But the Minister of Unemployment and Assimilation of the Québécois will not be freed.

3 The government decides to meet the six original demands of the FLQ. In this case Pierre Laporte and James Cross will be freed safe and sound within the twenty-four hours following the accomplishment in full of the liberation operation.

This communiqué is the last from the Chenier cell before the execution or liberation of Pierre Laporte. The whole situation is quite clear. Any obstinacy or delay will be considered a tacit refusal.

WE SHALL OVERCOME.

Front de libération du Québec.

P.S. We shall consider any slowness on the government's part in giving a definite reply to our demands as an inexcusable delay. We repeat that any hesitation will be considered as a refusal, any request for contact by communiqué or otherwise will be considered as a refusal.

You have in your hands the complete text in which the seven initial demands of the FLQ are mentioned.

The FLQ draftsmen and delivery boys were not the only one to work on

Monday, October 12. Joining the Vigilantes was the Front de la justice du Québec who, through the ruse of a false bomb threat at Place Bonaventure, left a note promising a "three for one" reprisal against the families of the "political prisoners" if Cross or Laporte were killed. In Petawawa troops began to move towards Ottawa, the 2nd Combat Group reaching Uplands Airport by helicopter at 5:30 PM and others arriving by convoy during the night. The next day prominent politicians walked the streets of Ottawa with armed troops at their sides. More troop movements were reported near Montreal, but officials continued to deny that they had anything to do with the crisis. In Quebec City the Nelson cell emerged with the threat that unless the medical specialists returned to work "one of those pigs will share our company for an indefinite period of time."

In Montreal Mr Bourassa continued to meet with his cabinet and advisers, and apparently discussed the crisis with the opposition leaders by telephone. At 7:15, presumably after consultation with Ottawa, he made the following statement:

> Following the offer of discussion made last night to the FLQ by the government of Quebec, the FLQ has decided, if we refer to a communiqué made public this morning, to name Mr Robert Lemieux as its representative.
>
> The government of Quebec has decided to name as its representative Mr Robert Demers ... a Montreal lawyer.
>
> Mr Demers will therefore represent the cabinet in discussion of the initial question which I mentioned in my broadcast yesterday. Mr Demers is ready to meet Mr Lemieux immediately after the broadcast of this communiqué.

Later that night Mr Demers met Lemieux in his cell. In court the next morning, Mr Lemieux refused to plead, arguing that the charge of obstruction was political; he was let out on his own recognizance. After a brief visit to the Lord Nelson Hotel – his headquarters, home, and studio – where with the ever-present Michel Chartrand he toasted "Québec libre," he was off to meet Bourassa and Demers. At least two meetings were held. Mr Bourassa admitted that he insisted that "There can be no question ... of the government accepting or discussing the FLQ demands before dealing with the initial question," that is, the safety of Cross and Laporte. Mr Lemieux suggested that the "political prisoners" be held captive in Cuba or Algeria and the ransom money kept in safekeeping until the host government was informed by Canadian authorities that Cross and Laporte were safe. Mr Demers apparently countered with the proposition that one member from each of the cells be held as hostage by the government until the prisoners were freed, on the promise that they would then be allowed to join their colleagues.

Following the evening meeting on October 13, Mr Lemieux terminated

La Presse, Montreal, October 15, 1970

the discussions. At another press conference at the Lord Nelson he declared that he would not meet Mr Demers again "without a new mandate" and charged that although Demers gave him the impression that the government seriously wished to negotiate, it was possible that it was only buying time. "I will not allow myself to be used in this way," he declared defiantly. At his side were Michel Chartrand, Charles Gagnon, and Pierre Vallières. Mr Chartrand shouted at a camera that given the situation in Quebec the kidnappers could not be condemned, and promised that the CNTU would provide bodyguards to protect such FLQ members from the Vigilantes: "If a single hair of a French Canadian is harmed by a vigilante, that will start the ball rolling. We're fed up."

Meanwhile, as police raids continued throughout the province, the Service Action cell emerged with a communiqué which read: "We will kill policemen who make raids without warrants in Quebec. There will be executions in Quebec if the conditions of liberation are not respected. Our cell will make only executions and destruction of police. Long live the patriots. FLQ." Police told reporters that the communiqué was believed to be legitimate.

"Well, just watch me"

In Ottawa on the evening of October 13 Mr Sharp admitted that Canadian officials had visited Cuba and Algeria to inform those governments of the FLQ demands, but also, one suspected, to see what arrangements could be made if negotiations were successfully carried out. However, the news was buried well under the report of an encounter between reporters Tim Ralfe of the CBC and Peter Reilly of CJOH-TV and Mr Trudeau as he entered the Commons that afternoon:

Q: Sir, what is it with all these men with guns around here?
A: Haven't you noticed?
Q: Yes, I've noticed them. I wondered why you people decided to have them.
A: What's your worry?
Q: I'm not worried, but you seem to be.
A: So if you're not worried, what's your ... I'm not worried.
Q: I'm worried about living in a town that's full of people with guns running around.
A: Why? Have they done anything to you? Have they pushed you around or anything?
Q: They've pushed around friends of mine.
A: Yes? What were your friends doing?
Q: Trying to take pictures of them.
A: Aha.
Q: Is that against the law?
A: No, not at all.
Q: Doesn't it worry you, having a town that you've got to resort to this kind of thing?
A: It doesn't worry me. I think it's natural that if people are being abducted that they be protected against such abductions. What would you do if a Quebec minister – another Quebec minister were abducted or a federal minister?
Q: But isn't that one of the ...
A: Is your position that you should give in to the seven demands of the FLQ and ... ?
Q: No, not at all. My position is completely the opposite.
A: What is your position?
Q: My position is that you don't give in to any of them.
A: All right. But you don't protect yourselves against the possibility of blackmail?
Q: Well, how can you protect everybody that is going to be a possible target without a much bigger military force, without putting somebody on everybody in the country, and turning it almost into a police state?
A: So, what do you suggest – that we protect nobody?
Q: How can you protect them all?
A: Well, you can't protect them all but are you therefore arguing that you shouldn't protect any?
Q: That's right.

A: That's your position?

Q: Right.

A: All right. So Pierre Laporte wasn't protected and he was abducted. If you had hindsight, would you not have preferred to protect him and Mr Cross?

Q: Well, second guessing is pretty easy, but you can't do it.

A: Well all right, but I'm asking you to first guess now.

Q: No, because it's impossible.

A: It would have been impossible to protect cabinet ministers of the provincial government or diplomats?

Q: I would suspect so, with all the diplomats there are in this country.

A: Well, we've got a big army.

Q: You're going to use it up pretty fast at this rate.

A: What do you mean at this rate?

Q: Six and seven.

[Reilly now questioning]

Q: If I could interpolate something here. You seem to be thinking, in your statement in the House this morning – you seemed to be saying that you thought the press had been less than responsible in its coverage of this story so far. Could you elaborate on that?

A: Not less than responsible. I was suggesting that they should perhaps use a bit more restraint which you're not doing now – you're going to make a big news item of this I am sure.

Q: Well, the papers – it is a big news item.

A: Yes, but the main thing that the FLQ is trying to gain from this is a hell of a lot of publicity for the movement.

Q: A recognition.

A: Yes and I am suggesting that the more recognition you give to them the greater the victory is, and I'm not interested in giving them a victory.

Q: ... the proposition that perhaps it would be wise to use less inflammatory terms than "bandits" when you talk about a bunch of people who have the lives of two men in their hands?

A: You don't think they're bandits?

Q: Well, regardless of what I think, I don't think I would be inclined to wave a red flag in their face if they held two of my friends or colleagues with guns at their heads.

A: Well, first of all, I didn't call them bandits. I called the people who were in jail now bandits, who had been tried before the law and condemned to a prison term and I said that you people should stop calling them political prisoners. They're not political prisoners, they're outlaws. They're criminal prisoners, they're not political prisoners, and they're bandits. That's why they're in jail.

[Ralfe now questioning]

Q: But with your army troops you seem to be combatting them almost as though it is a war, and if it is a war does anything that they say have validity?

A: Don't be silly. We're not combatting them as if it's war but we're using some of the army as peace agents in order that the police be more free to do their job as policemen and not spend their time guarding your friends against some form of kidnapping.

Q: You said earlier that you would protect them in this way but you have said before that this kind of violence, what you're fighting here, the kind of violence of the FLQ, can lead to a police state.

A: Sure. That's what you're complaining about, isn't it?

Q: Well yes, but surely that decision is yours, not the FLQ's.

A: Yes, but I've asked you what your own logic is. It's to let them abduct anybody and not give any protection to anyone – call off the police, that seems to be your position.

Q: Not call off the police. Surely the police's job is to catch people who break the law.

A: Yes, but not to give protection to those citizens who might be blackmailed for one reason or another?

Q: Which must be half of the population of the country, in one way or another. I explained it badly I think, but what you're talking about to me is choices, and my choice is to live in a society that is free and democratic, which means that you don't have people with guns running around in it.

A: Correct.

Q: And one of the things I have to give up for that choice is the fact that people like you may be kidnapped.

A: Sure, but this isn't my choice, obviously. You know, I think it is more important to get rid of those who are committing violence against the total society and those who are trying to run the government through a parallel power by establishing their authority by kidnapping and blackmail. And I think it is our duty as a government to protect government officials and important people in our society against being used as tools in this blackmail. Now, you don't agree to this but I am sure that, once again with hindsight, you would probably have found it preferable if Mr Cross and Mr Laporte had been protected from kidnapping, which they weren't because these steps we're taking now weren't taken. But even with your hindsight I don't see how you can deny that.

Q: No, I still go back to the choice that you have to make in the kind of society that you live in.

A: Yes, well there are a lot of bleeding hearts around who just don't like to see people with helmets and guns. All I can say is, go on and bleed, but it is more important to keep law and order in the society than to be worried about weak-kneed people who don't like the looks of ...

Q: At any cost? How far would you go with that? How far would you extend that?

A: Well, just watch me.

Q: At reducing civil liberties? To what extent?

A: To what extent?

Q: Well, if you extend this and you say, OK, you're going to do anything to protect them, does this include wire-tapping, reducing other civil liberties in some way?

A: Yes, I think the society must take every means at its disposal to defend itself against the emergence of a parallel power which defies the elected power in this country and I think that goes to any distance. So long as there is a power in here which is challenging the elected representative of the people, I think that power must be stopped and I think it's only, I repeat, weak-kneed bleeding hearts who are afraid to take these measures.

Q: Excuse me, sir, you have been largely silent on this whole case and understandably so. If you had anything to address to the abductors at this point, what would it be?

A: I think Mr Bourassa stated the position yesterday, and I repeated it in the House, with which we agree completely. There is only one thing now that we are prepared to talk to them about. It's a way in which Mr Cross and Mr Laporte can be effectively released. This mechanism has to be dealt with first and foremost.

Thank you, sir.

In Montreal that afternoon Mr Demers and Mr Lemieux met again, and the latter then went to Quebec where a special session of the National Assembly had been called to deal with the doctors' strike. Lemieux refused to go, but told the press that the slowness of the negotiations endangered the lives of the hostages. The FLQ responded to his news con-

Le rendez-vous électronique

Le Devoir, Montreal, October 16, 1970

ferences by issuing a joint communiqué at 5 AM on October 14, again through Pierre Pascau of CKLM:

Communiqué no 9, Chenier cell – Liberation cell.
October 14, 1970, 5 AM.

After a meeting and agreement between the Chenier cell and the Liberation cell, the Front de libération du Québec (Liberation cell) wants to underline the following points as a result of the news conference by lawyer Lemieux on the outcome of talks with the ruling authorities.

1 Regarding the guarantees asked of us by the ruling authorities, the Front de libération du Québec can only renew its solemn commitment before the people of Quebec.

There is no question, as suggested by the ruling authorities, of turning over to them a member of each cell, as guarantees. However, we accept as a last solution Mr Lemieux's proposal to the effect that the country which welcomes the political prisoners should hold them (as well as the $500,000) until we have freed J. Cross and P. Laporte alive and well.

2 We seriously question the goodwill of the authorities concerned. What "guarantees" can they offer us concerning the end of the searches, raids, and arrests by their fascist political police? For more than eight days the repressive police forces, on orders of Choquette's dirty dogs, have increased their illegal raids and arrests despite the fact that that was one of the principal conditions for the release (alive and well) of J. Cross and P. Laporte.

After so many illegal actions by their "bouncers" how will the ruling authorities be able to say to us with any conviction that their fascist political police will momentarily stop their "hunt"?

How can we believe that the ruling authorities want to save the life of J. Cross, P. Laporte, when they order their "bouncers" to find the abductors, when they know that our arrest means immediate death for the diplomat and for the Minister of Unemployment and of Assimilation?

3 The Front de libération du Québec doesn't ask for a "guarantee" from Mr Lemieux concerning his integrity and good faith!

We renew the mandate of lawyer Lemieux as regarding the fulfilment of our conditions and we give him "carte blanche" to negotiate the aforementioned conditions.

4 As before lawyer Robert Lemieux must report publicly the results of negotiations which will be carried on during the course of the day, Wednesday.

5 Following the results, we will issue a new communiqué. We will let lawyer Lemieux as well as the ruling authorities know our decision and we will set a last deadline for the fulfilment of our demands.

We shall overcome.

Front de libération du Québec.

Note 1: we want to remind the ruling authorities that there is no question of either one or several members of the Front giving themselves up to their "bouncers." Any new proposal regarding this will be considered as negative and will only endanger J. Cross' and Pierre Laporte's chances.

Note 2: we ask lawyer Lemieux to give a detailed account of past and present police operations (searches, raids, arrests, and torture).

Note 3: would you please give a copy of this communiqué to lawyer Robert Lemieux.

“It’s war—total war”

OCTOBER 14–16

TROOPS continued to move to Camp Bouchard, twenty-five miles from Montreal, on October 14. In Toronto Prime Minister John Robarts rejected any deal with the FLQ – “It’s war – total war.” In Paris a group calling itself the European contingent of the FLQ boldly threatened to destroy Canadian air and rail communications outside of Quebec. In Quebec the press continued its speculations. Claude Ryan and some others believed that the Quebec cabinet, although badly divided, was anxious to go to almost any length to secure the release of Cross and Laporte but were held in check by an inflexible Canadian government. Claude Henault wrote in the Toronto *Telegram* (October 15):

A source close to Quebec Premier Robert Bourassa said in an interview yesterday that Mr. Bourassa, who was elected on a pro-Federal ticket, is “dead tired from lack of sleep in the past few days and getting a little fed up with Ottawa’s refusal to be flexible.”

Ottawa, the source said, seems unable to see the problem from Quebec’s point of view. Mr. Bourassa is under considerable pressure, partly from within the easily-split Quebec Liberal Federation, to obtain the freedom of the kidnapped Labor Minister Pierre Laporte.

Prime Minister Bourassa repeatedly denied that there was any basic split in the cabinet, and both he and Mr Trudeau denied that Quebec was being driven by a hard line from Ottawa. (Indeed, the evidence suggests that Trudeau was restraining Quebec and Montreal authorities from precipitately demanding the use of the army or the War Measures Act.) Nevertheless, the view that Ottawa was determining policy and that outside pressure would stiffen the supposedly floundering Bourassa cabinet lay behind the meeting of sixteen prominent Québécois at the Holiday Inn on October 14. Claude Ryan (*Le Devoir*, October 30) provided the background to the meeting:

... On Wednesday October 14 Mr Bourassa phoned and told me there might be “a small step” in the direction of taking a firm stand. His remarks caused me some concern. On the same day at about 5 PM I received a telephone call from Mr René Lévesque. The latter, who had been following the line adopted by the *Devoir* during this crisis with some interest, told me that he feared a shift in Mr Bourassa's attitude and asked me whether I would be prepared to join several other individuals in publishing a joint statement aimed at supporting the intention announced three days earlier by Mr Bourassa, that is, to try to find a solution by negotiation. It was the first time I had spoken to Mr Lévesque since the election of April 29. Because I wished to do everything possible to save Laporte's and Cross' lives I accepted this invitation, I helped in preparing the final text of the "joint statement," and I was at the press conference (October 14, 9 PM) when this statement was made public ...

The document read as follows:

The Cross-Laporte affair is primarily a Quebec drama. One of the two hostages is a citizen of Quebec, the other a diplomat whose functions made him a temporary citizen with the same rights to respect for his life and to his dignity as a man as us all.

On the other hand, the people of the FLQ are a marginal section of this same Quebec. But they still form part of our reality, because extremism is a part of the social structure, even if it indicates a serious condition and can put that social structure in mortal peril.

The destiny of two human lives, the reputation and collective honour of our society, the obvious danger of a political and social degradation that this society is presently facing, all this makes it clear to us that the responsibility for finding a solution and applying it quite rightly lies primarily with Quebec.

We feel that certain attitudes outside Quebec, the last and most unbelievable of which was that of Premier Robarts of Ontario, plus the rigid – almost military – atmosphere we see in Ottawa, runs the risk of reducing Quebec and its government to tragic ineffectualness. Superhuman effort [is needed] to agree to bargain and compromise. In this respect, we believe that Quebec and its government really hold the responsibility and the moral mandate, and are the real custodians of the facts and the climate of opinion which allow them to make knowledgeable decisions.

Especially as, particularly in certain non-Quebec quarters, we fear the terrible temptation of the worst type of politics, in other words the idea that Quebec in chaos and disorder would at last be easy to control by any available means.

This is why, forgetting the difference of opinion we have on a number of subjects, solely conscious for the moment of being Québécois and therefore totally involved, we wish to give our complete support to the intention announced Sunday evening by the Bourassa government, which means basically our strongest support for negotiating an exchange of the two hostages for the political prisoners. This must be accomplished despite and against all obstruction from outside Quebec, which necessarily implies the positive co-operation of the federal government.

And we urgently invite all the citizens who share our point of view to make it known publicly as quickly as possible.

The signatories of the statement are: René Lévesque, president of the Parti québécois; Alfred Rouleau, president of l'Assurance-vie-Desjardins; Marcel Pépin, president of CSN; Louis Laberge, president of the FTQ [Fédération des travailleurs du Québec]; Jean-Marc Kirouac, president of the UCC [Union catholique des cultivateurs]; Claude Ryan, director of *Le Devoir*; Jacques Parizeau, president of the executive council of the Parti québécois; Fernand

Daoust, secretary general of the FTQ; Yvan Charbonneau, president of the CEQ [Corporation des enseignants du Québec]; Mathias Rioux, president of l'Alliance des professeurs of Montreal; Camille Laurin, parliamentary leader of the Parti québécois; Guy Rocher, sociology professor at l'Université de Montréal; Fernand Dumont, director of l'Institut supérieur des sciences humaines at l'Université Laval; Paul Bélanger, political science professor at l'Université Laval; Raymond Laliberté, ex-president of CEQ; Marcel Rioux, anthropology professor at l'Université de Montréal.

The same evening in Quebec City Prime Minister Bourassa declared that the cabinet had not taken a final stand on terms to be negotiated with the FLQ. The primary question, he explained, echoing a statement made by Mr Trudeau in the Commons the day before, was to find a mechanism whereby the government could be assured of the safety of Cross and Laporte if any demands were to be met.

By October 14 the flood of communiqués, the flow of press conferences, the apparent emergence of new cells, the daily bomb scares in Montreal, and the stories of caches of arms and more arms thefts had led to increasingly outspoken demands for new initiatives to achieve results. The Prime Minister was pressed in the House by Robert Stanfield:

Mr. Speaker, I wish to ask the Prime Minister whether, in view of statements he made outside the House yesterday, consideration is being given to the declaring of emergency police powers of the sort, for example, to permit the police to search without warrant and arrest and hold individuals for questioning without having to lay a specific charge or justify any such action? Is any such consideration being given?

Right Hon. P. E. Trudeau (Prime Minister): Since the beginning of this emergency, Mr. Speaker, the government has considered all possible types of action including this and many others, but there has been no decision made along these or any other lines which is not obvious to the country and to Parliament.

Mr. Stanfield: Will the Prime Minister give the House the assurance that no action of this nature will be taken without the approval of the House of Commons?

Mr. Trudeau: I believe, Mr. Speaker, that this is a matter of law. Quite frankly, I do not think this type of suspension of civil liberties, if I understand the Leader of the Opposition, would be possible without some amendment to our statute or some action by the government which would have to be brought before the House at some point.

Mr. Stanfield: Will the Prime Minister give the assurance that even if the government has this authority in law no such action will be taken without seeking the approval of the House of Commons?

Mr. Trudeau: This is completely hypothetical. I repeat that if such action were ever contemplated it would certainly be discussed in the House of Commons. Whether it would be immediately before or immediately after would depend, of course, on –

Some hon. Members: Oh, Oh!

Mr. Trudeau: I am sorry to observe the lightness with which the opposition treats this question. It is obvious that if urgent action is needed at some time in the middle of the night we cannot ask Parliament to approve it first.

Mr. Bell: All these things happen in the middle of the night.

Mr. Diefenbaker: You have no power to do it except through Parliament.

That night a cabinet committee, apparently consisting of Trudeau, Turner, Macdonald, and McIlraith, met for three hours to discuss strategy. The next day in the Commons the Prime Minister admitted that the government had "considered every possible way in which the government of Canada, in conjunction with the government of Quebec, could meet this very difficult situation," including the War Measures Act.

The Army Summoned

As Thursday, October 15, dawned, the pressure in Montreal became almost unbearable. The previous evening Robert Lemieux and his friends had addressed a rally of one thousand students at the Université de Montréal and urged them to boycott classes. Operation Débrayage (Walkout) began the next day. A campaign to organize a general student strike in support of the FLQ began at the Université de Montréal, where the four horsemen – Lemieux, Chartrand, Vallières, and Gagnon – addressed a mass rally before moving off to other campuses. The social science students voted to strike, but the law students decided to wait upon events. The largest CEGEP, Vieux Montréal, held an all-day teach-in to study the FLQ manifesto. At the Université du Québec students occupied the administrative offices and promised to keep the campus closed until the six demands of the kidnappers had been met. A press release stated that "The special secretariat of the student occupation will occupy the office of the rector until the victory of the FLQ." Resolutions passed at the student rallies were to be placed before a mass rally that evening at the Paul Sauvé Arena, after which the rally organizers planned a march through the streets to the Hôtel de Ville and the Palais de Justice.

As the police faced the prospect of mass street demonstrations and checked innumerable bomb threats – one such threat forced the evacuation of the Palais de Justice in the morning – Prime Minister Bourassa decided to call in the army. At 3:07, after discussions with the opposition leaders, who concurred, he made a statement in the National Assembly:

> ... As I have already stated and I repeat it today, our aim is to make every effort possible under the circumstances to save these two lives, without in so doing opening the way to anarchy.
>
> A short time ago a statement from the government asking for military support was made public. During a press conference given by me yesterday

It's Tommy this an' Tommy that, an' "Chuck 'im out, the brute!"
but it's saviour of 'is country, when the guns begin to shoot.—Kipling

Toronto Daily Star, October 16, 1970

evening I indicated that we were asking a lot of our police force, in view of the unusual and extensive efforts required in order to protect the population and public buildings, and I said that we could not carry on indefinitely asking this force to ensure the protection of everyone involved under the present limitations, for this would be beyond their capabilities.

We have therefore asked for military support so that the police force may be able to continue protecting public buildings and the population.

Mr Speaker, I am asking for the co-operation of all members and all parties – and it might be said that I am sure in advance of receiving this co-operation. Democratic rule in Quebec is being threatened at this time. This democratic rule for which tens of thousands of individuals have given their lives over a period of time within our province is now in danger, and our prime responsibility is to save it. It is with this in mind, in order to save these human lives and to save a régime for which millions of people have died that, in co-operation with all members, we mean to assume our responsibilities ...

Within minutes troops were on the Assembly grounds in Quebec, and in less than an hour they were landing by helicopter at the St Hubert air base and taking up positions at strategic buildings in Montreal. More than one thousand soldiers reached Montreal on October 15, and more were to follow. In the afternoon the Bourassa government also passed an order-in-council which placed all police and army personnel under the command of Maurice Saint-Pierre, the director of the Quebec Provincial Police.

As the troops took up their positions throughout the city Robert Lemieux used the television cameras to speak to his "chers patriotes":

I have very, very serious information that police have found the Chenier cell and are only waiting to find the Liberation cell which holds James Cross before attacking with force to free the two men. I received this information last night from a very serious businessman who heard it from a cabinet minister of the Quebec government. While I am not absolutely certain whether the information is well-founded, I take it very, very, very seriously ...

I demand an answer from the government as to whether or not this information is well-founded ... If the government feels this information imperils the hostages, let it hurry up and answer me. I consider it my duty to tell the whole truth. Besides, if the police act it will mean the death of several people. I don't want to bear the moral responsibility for those deaths by remaining silent.

With that injection of new fuel into the crisis, Mr Lemieux raced off to address another rally.

In Quebec City Mr Bourassa and the cabinet met again and soon after 9 PM, with Ottawa's agreement, made the following statement:

Faced with the deterioration of the situation and the need to ensure public order, the government of Quebec has decided to give its final viewpoint in its negotiations with the Front de libération du Québec.

In the matter of the initial question, the freeing safe and sound of Mr Laporte and Mr Cross, the government of Quebec suggests that either the International Red Cross or the Consulate of Cuba in Montreal act as intermediary between the two parties.

As for the other conditions set by the Front de libération du Québec, the government replies as follows:

1 It does not accept the freeing of the total number of prisoners listed by the Front de libération du Québec. However, it promises to recommend firmly the parole of five [Demers, Faulkner, LaQuerre, Simard, and R. Lévesque] of the prisoners who have asked for parole. It has already undertaken steps in this direction.

2 The authorities concerned promise to furnish safe passage to members of the FLQ cells who carried out the kidnapping of Mr Laporte and Mr Cross.

3 The same authorities are disposed to assure themselves that there will be a plane for the purpose of transport to the chosen country.

4 Finally, in regard to the other conditions, the government does not believe it would be legitimate to accept them.

The government took this decision in weighing all the implications and alternatives which could exist.

Because of the nature of the situation and the numerous delays which already exist, the government requests a reply within six hours of the publication of this communiqué.

Lawyer Robert Lemieux has been advised of the content of this communiqué by lawyer Robert Demers.

The die had been cast. Mr Bourassa's statement brought an angry Mr Lemieux quickly back to his studio at the Lord Nelson. Enraged, he strode before the television cameras and microphones. Naming the men who had signed the Holiday Inn declaration, he declared that they represented the public will in Quebec, whereas "In offering to free five good Quebec guys who should have been parolled a long time ago anyway, and whose paroles are coming soon, the government is simply mocking the people of Quebec. I urge the government to meet, not in the next few hours, but in minutes, and to reconsider. Reconsider this ... this incredible mockery. My mandate has ended. I have nothing more to say."

Asked if he was walking out of the negotiations, Mr Lemieux replied: "I've been thrown out on my ass." He then raced off to the Paul Sauvé Arena to hear Mr Vallières tell the three thousand present that "the government claim the FLQ is a small band of criminals ... But you are the FLQ, you and all the popular groups that fight for the liberation of Quebec. We must organize the fight for liberation in every district, in each plant, in each office, everywhere."

As Lemieux fanned the flames of civil disorder, Claude Ryan finished his October 16 editorial, brooding over the dangers to democracy and civil order in Quebec and supporting the use of the army:

If there is any lesson to be learned from the heavy day we had yesterday, it is that in many respects the two hostages whose lives are at stake in the Cross-Laporte affair are for some people like pawns on a much bigger chessboard.

Whereas well-intended citizens were striving to limit the bets at stake as much as possible and to encourage settlement by negotiation, others spent their time in spreading the fire, to create the impression (unfortunately this is artificial and closer to the workings of "mob rule" than true democracy) of a general attack on the establishment. Places which should have fostered democracy have once again become filled with constraint, ideological conformity of the worst kind, and even fear. It is as though while pretending to wish to negotiate we were trying to bring about an enormous collision.

The meetings and lock-out strikes which have increased in number over the past twenty-four hours confirm the analysis made by those for whom the problem posed by the FLQ goes quite a way beyond the narrow framework of illegal acts committed by some members of this organization. There is a very considerable political and social phenomenon in the events of the past few days. If you try to understand it by just looking at it through the magnifying glass of the Criminal Code, you are bypassing the main issue.

But all this upset raises another very serious problem for the authorities in charge of public law and order. To avoid a catastrophe Bourassa's government yesterday called on the Canadian Armed Forces for help. This gesture was saddening, but necessary nevertheless.

Police forces, who have been on the alert for almost two weeks, are on the verge of exhaustion. Fresh problems created by the FLQ's recent tactics have increased the work-load, necessitated longer periods of duty, and forced the guardians of law and order to remain continually on the lookout.

When confronted with the appeal made in the streets by Mr Lemieux and his friends, the Quebec government, with the experience of the past few years in mind, judged it necessary to call in the armed forces. And quite rightly so. To do otherwise would have been to overlook its duty.

It is always humiliating for a civil government to have to call upon the army when faced with situations in which the regular police should be all that is required. Add to that the fact that, in Quebec's case, there is a further complication, because of the fact that the army is commanded by the government in Ottawa under our federal system ...

... What happened yesterday might well be an intermediate step only. It is to be hoped that this will be all that is required and that we don't need to go any further. How can we forget, though, that it might be followed tomorrow by an even graver move, namely the implementation of the War Measures Act? I don't need to add that, should this come to pass, that's it, for we don't know how long, as far as the prime responsibility of the Quebec government is concerned, and all political authority and initiative would be taken over by the central government.

Such an outlook does not cease to worry us. This country – and the forces able to support it across the continent in time of need – is still strong enough to prevent Quebec from sliding down into anarchy and a dictatorship under the yoke of powers bent on demagogy and destruction. If Quebec wants to achieve greater liberty, or even independence, it must, in order to obtain the support of world opinion, do so by democratic means. Otherwise, to prevent it being taken over by the leftist totalitarianism, many people will think about trampling it under the all too familiar boot – alas – of a power which is alien to its culture, and from which it quite rightly wants to be free.

We must at all cost avoid the downfall of Quebec into civil war and its subjugation to martial law. But this will only be possible if the legitimate government of Quebec manages to assert its moral authority more firmly and to broaden its basic support among the people over the next few weeks.

The War Measures Act

The men responsible for public policy were even more aware of the gravity of the situation in Montreal. Undoubtedly Bourassa's final appeal and the deadline were the result of an agreement with Ottawa. The order-in-council proclaiming the War Measures Act and the emergency regulations must already have been written. According to most reports the federal cabinet had met on the afternoon of October 15 and agreed to the use of the War Measures Act if the deteriorating situation in Montreal did not change and the FLQ made no response to Mr Bourassa's last-minute appeal. At 10:30 PM the Prime Minister informed the leaders of the opposition parties of the action to be undertaken and at 3 AM on October 16 he received the following letters from Quebec and Montreal requesting emergency measures:

Government of Quebec
The Prime Minister
Quebec City, October 16, 1970

Mr Prime Minister,

During the last few days the people of Quebec have been greatly shocked by the kidnapping of Mr. James R. Cross, representative of the British Government in Montreal, and the Hon. Pierre Laporte, Minister of Labour and Manpower and Minister of Immigration of Quebec, as well as by the threats to the security of the state and individuals expressed in communiqués issued by the Front de Libération du Québec or on its behalf, and finally by all the circumstances surrounding these events.

After consultation with authorities directly responsible for the administration of justice in Quebec, the Quebec Government is convinced that the law, as it stands now, is inadequate to meet this situation satisfactorily.

Under the circumstances, on behalf of the Government of Quebec, I request that emergency powers be provided as soon as possible so that more effective steps may be taken. I request particularly that such powers encompass the authority to apprehend and keep in custody individuals who, the Attorney General of Quebec has valid reasons to believe, are determined to overthrow the government through violence and illegal means. According to the information we have and which is available to you, we are facing a concerted effort to intimidate and overthrow the government and the democratic institutions of this province through planned and systematic illegal action, including insurrection. It is obvious that those participating in this concerted effort completely reject the principle of freedom under the rule of law.

The Quebec Government is convinced that such powers are necessary to meet the present emergency. Not only are two completely innocent men threatened with death, but we are also faced with an attempt by a minority to destroy social order through criminal action; it is for those reasons that our government is making the present request.

The government is confident that, through such powers, it will be able to put an immediate stop to intimidation and terror and to ensure peace and security for all citizens.

Please accept, Mr. Prime Minister, my very best regards.

Robert Bourassa.

City of Montreal, Canada
Office of the Chairman of
the Executive Committee
October 15, 1970

Mr. Prime Minister,

The chief of the Montreal Police Service has informed us that the means available to him are proving inadequate and that the assistance of higher levels of government has become essential for the protection of society against the seditious plot and the apprehended insurrection in which the recent kidnappings were the first step.

We are forwarding as a matter of the utmost urgency the report describing the scope of the threat and the urgent need to reinforce the machinery to cope with it.

We ask for every measure of assistance the federal government may deem useful and desirable in order to carry out the task of protecting society and the lives of citizens in this difficult period.

Lucien Saulnier
Chairman of the
Executive Committee

Jean Drapeau
Mayor of Montreal

October 15, 1970
Gentlemen:

An extremely dangerous subversive movement has progressively developed in Quebec in recent years with the objective of overthrowing the legitimate state by means of sedition and eventually armed insurrection.

The recent kidnappings of a foreign diplomat and a Crown minister of the province have signalled the launching by this movement of their seditious projects and acts leading directly to the insurrection and the overthrow of the state.

Under these circumstances, the investigation which the police authorities must undertake must necessarily delve into all aspects of the activities of the networks of this seditious movement, and should not be restricted to simply searching for the individuals who perpetrated the odious kidnapping of the two people who are still prisoners – for this would mean failure.

The threat served on society by this seditious conspiracy, which has moved into action in the past eleven days, the difficulties of investigating an organization split up into manifold tiny cells, each impervious to the others, and the unbelievable amount of checking and researching imposed on us have taxed, and continue to tax the resources our police force has at its disposal to their limit.

Considering how extremely urgent it is to achieve concrete results and unmask all the ramifications of this movement and its seditious activities, considering the volume and complexity of the proofs which must be collected and preserved, considering, finally, the enormity of the task we must accomplish, without moving into a repression which would be neither healthy nor desirable, the help of higher governments is essential to the completion of our job.

The slowness of procedures and the restraints imposed by the legal methods and mechanisms now at our disposal do not allow us at this time to cope with the situation.

Consequently, I recommend that the executive committee of the city request that the higher governments give us all the means they think appropriate and useful, so as to allow us to collect and present the proofs needed to protect society from the seditious and insurrectional manœuvres unleashed by the kidnappings.

Please accept, gentlemen, the expression of my most distinguished sentiments.

The Director
M. St-Pierre

The War Measures Act and the following regulations were approved at 4 AM. Police were on their way in Montreal well before 5:17 when the Prime Minister's Office issued a formal statement that the act had been proclaimed:

Whereas the War Measures Act provides that the issue of a proclamation under the authority of the governor-in-council shall be conclusive evidence that insurrection, real or apprehended, exists and has existed for any period of time therein stated and its continuance, until by the issue of a further proclamation it is declared that the insurrection no longer exists.

And whereas there is in contemporary Canadian society an element or group known as Le Front de Libération du Québec who advocate and resort to the use of force and the commission of criminal offences, including murder, threats of murder and kidnapping, as a means of or as an aid in accomplishing a governmental change within Canada and whose activities have given rise to a state of apprehended insurrection within the province of Quebec.

Therefore, His Excellency the Governor-General-in-Council, on the recommendation of the prime minister, is pleased to direct that a proclamation be issued proclaiming that apprehended insurrection exists and has existed as and from the fifteenth day of October, one thousand nine hundred and seventy.

Public Order Regulations, 1970
October 16, 1970

Whereas it continues to be recognized in Canada that men and institutions remain free only when freedom is founded upon respect for moral and spiritual values and the rule of law;

And whereas there is in contemporary Canadian society an element or group known as Le Front de Libération du Québec who advocate the use of force or the commission of crime as a means of or as an aid in accomplishing a governmental change within Canada and who have resorted to the commission of serious crimes including murder, threat of murder and kidnapping;

And whereas the government of Canada desires to ensure that lawful and effective measures can be taken against those who thus seek to destroy the basis of our democratic governmental system on which the enjoyment of our human rights and fundamental freedoms is founded and to ensure the continued protection of those rights and freedoms in Canada;

Therefore, His Excellency the Governor-General-in-Council, on the recommendation of the prime minister, pursuant to the War Measures Act, is pleased hereby to make the annexed regulations, to provide emergency powers for the preservation of public order in Canada.

REGULATIONS TO PROVIDE EMERGENCY POWERS FOR THE PRESERVATION OF PUBLIC ORDER IN CANADA

Short Title

1 These regulations may be cited as the Public Order Regulations, 1970.

Interpretation

2 In these regulations,

"communicate" includes the act of communicating by telephone, broadcasting or other audible or visible means;

"peace officer" means a peace officer as defined in the Criminal Code and includes a member of the Canadian Armed Forces;

"statements" includes words spoken or written or recorded electronically or electromagnetically or otherwise, and gestures, signs or other visible representations; and

"the unlawful association" means the group of persons or association declared by these regulations to be an unlawful association.

3 The group of persons or association known as Le Front de Libération du Québec and any successor group or successor association of the said Le Front de Libération du Québec, or any group of persons or association that advocates the use of force or the commission of crime as a means of or as an aid in accomplishing governmental change within Canada is declared to be an unlawful association.

4 A person who

a. is or professes to be a member of the unlawful association,

b. acts or professes to act as an officer of the unlawful association,

c. communicates statements on behalf of or as a representative or professed representative of the unlawful association,

d. advocates or promotes the unlawful acts, aims, principles or policies of the unlawful association,

e. contributes anything as dues or otherwise to the unlawful association or to anyone for the benefit of the unlawful association,

f. solicits subscriptions or contributions for the unlawful association, or

g. advocates, promotes or engages in the use of force or the commission of criminal offences as a means of accomplishing a governmental change within Canada is guilty of an indictable offence and liable to imprisonment for a term not exceeding five years.

5 A person who, knowing or having reasonable cause to believe that another

Winnipeg Free Press, December 29, 1970

person is guilty of an offence under these regulations, gives that other person any assistance with intent thereby to prevent, hinder or interfere with the apprehension, trial or punishment of that person for that offence is guilty of an indictable offence and liable to imprisonment for a term not exceeding five years.

6 An owner, lessee, agent or superintendent of any building, room, premises or other place who knowingly permits therein any meeting of the unlawful association or any branch, committee or members thereof, or any assemblage

of persons who promote the acts, aims, principles or policies of the unlawful association is guilty of an indictable offence and liable to a fine of not more than five thousand dollars or to imprisonment for a term not exceeding five years or to both.

7 1. A person arrested for an offence under section 4 shall be detained in custody without bail pending trial unless the attorney-general of the province in which the person is being detained consents to the release of that person on bail.

2. Where an accused has been arrested for an offence under these regulations and is detained in custody for the purpose only of ensuring his attendance at the trial of the charge under these regulations in respect of which he is in custody and the trial has not commenced within ninety days from the time he was first detained, the person having the custody of the accused shall, forthwith upon the expiration of such ninety days, apply to a judge of the superior court of criminal jurisdiction in the province in which the accused is being detained to fix a date for the trial and the judge may fix a date for the beginning of the trial or give such directions as he thinks necessary for expediting the trial of the accused.

8 In any prosecution for an offence under these regulations, evidence that any person

a. attended any meeting of the unlawful association,

b. spoke publicly in advocacy for the unlawful association, or

c. communicated statements of the unlawful association as a representative or professed representative of the unlawful association is, in the absence of evidence to the contrary, proof that he is a member of the unlawful association.

9 1. A peace officer may arrest without warrant

a. a person who he has reason to suspect is a member of the unlawful association; or

b. a person who professes to be a member of the unlawful association; or

c. a person who he has reason to suspect has committed, is committing or is about to commit an act described in paragraphs *b.* to *g.* of section 4.

2. A person arrested pursuant to subsection 1 shall be taken before a justice having jurisdiction and charged with an offence described in section 4 not later than seven days after his arrest, unless the attorney-general of the province in which the person is being detained has, before the expiry of those seven days, issued an order that the accused be further detained until the expiry of a period not exceeding twenty-one days after his arrest, at the end of which period the person arrested shall be taken before a justice having jurisdiction and charged with an offence described in section 4 or released from custody.

10 A peace officer may enter and search without warrant any premises, place, vehicle, vessel or aircraft in which he has reason to suspect

a. anything is kept or used for the purpose of promoting the unlawful acts, aims, principles or policies of the unlawful association;

b. there is anything that may be evidence of an offence under these regulations;

c. any member of the unlawful association is present; or

d. any person is being detained by the unlawful association.

11 Any property that a peace officer has reason to suspect may be evidence of an offence under these regulations may, without warrant, be seized by a

peace officer and held for ninety days from the date of seizure or until the final disposition of any proceedings in relation to an offence under these regulations in which such property may be required, whichever is the later.

12 These regulations shall be enforced in such manner and by such courts, officers and authorities as enforce indictable offences created by the Criminal Code.

By the time the House of Commons met on the morning of October 16 more than 150 suspected members of the FLQ had been detained and another hundred were picked up before nightfall. Among the more prominent were Pierre Vallières, Charles Gagnon, Robert Lemieux, Jacques Larue-Langlois, Dr Serge Mongeau, Gérard Godin (an editor of *Québec-Presse*), and his friend Pauline Julien, and Ronald Labelle, a journalist who had interviewed two FLQ terrorists training in Jordan. Before the House met the Prime Minister briefed the Liberal caucus, and when it opened immediately tabled the Bourassa-Drapeau correspondence.

The Government Explains

Mr Trudeau justified the government's action on the grounds of the deterioration of the situation in Quebec and as a response to the appeal from Quebec. The use of the act, he declared, was "only an interim and ... somewhat unsatisfactory measure" and he promised that the government intended to discuss with opposition leaders "the desirability of introducing legislation of a less comprehensive nature." The Prime Minister frankly admitted his sympathy with those who were concerned about the suspension of civil liberties under the act, and promised that the powers would be withdrawn "as soon as it has been demonstrated that there is a cessation of the violence and the threats of violence which made necessary their introduction." He reminded the House that

> ... this extreme position into which governments have been forced is in some respects a trap. It is a well known technique of revolutionary groups who attempt to destroy society by unjustified violence to goad the authorities into inflexible attitudes. The revolutionaries then employ this evidence of alleged authoritarianism as justification for the need to use violence in their renewed attacks on the social structure. I appeal to all Canadians not to become so obsessed by what the government has done today in response to terrorism that they forget the opening play in this vicious game. That play was taken by the revolutionaries; they chose to use bombing, murder and kidnapping.

Mr Stanfield quickly observed that while the Prime Minister informed him of the likely action and provided an opportunity for discussion, he had in no way given his approval; on the other hand, he was unwilling to say that he did not approve, for the government alone was in a position to know whether there was a real or apprehended insurrection and the government alone had to bear the responsibility for such a serious suspension of civil liberties. New Democratic party leader T. C. Douglas was more forthright: "In my opinion the government has overreacted to what is undoubtedly a critical situation. Does civil disturbance constitute apprehended insurrection? ... Mr. Speaker, we are not prepared to use the preservation of law and order as a smokescreen to destroy the liberties and the freedom of the people of Canada ... The government, I submit, is using a sledgehammer to crack a peanut." Friday, October 16, he concluded, would be looked upon "as a black Friday for civil liberties in Canada." Réal Caouette was unequivocal: Messrs Stanfield and Douglas were playing politics; the government had been remiss in not acting years before to root out radicals and separatists; and the War Measures Act was overdue.

The major explanation and defence of government policy was left to John Turner, minister of justice:

> The government of Canada has to take the final responsibility, but when the Government of the Province of Quebec and the mayor of the largest city in this country, on the information available to them and the information available to us through our own law enforcement agencies, are of the opinion that the state has been reached where we ought to, as sound and commonsense human beings, anticipate a danger to our society in the form of insurrection and are willing to use that type of vocabulary to the Prime Minister of Canada, then that is material which we cannot ignore.
>
> I want to recite a list of events that have contributed to the rapid acceleration of this dangerous situation in Quebec. They are the kidnappings, which in themselves if they were isolated would be a purely criminal affair but, within the context of a wider conspiracy and being used for ransom against a legitimately constituted government, are something else. We have the continuous threats to life and property in the communications of the FLQ of a seditious, violent and inflammatory nature. They have been issued and members are aware of them.
>
> We have also a series of bombings and violence, a rising increase in thefts of dynamite now available in some hidden caches in the province of Quebec. More disturbing, we have a type of erosion of the public will in the feeling among some sincere people that an exchange of prisoners for the victims of the kidnappings would somehow ease the situation.
>
> ... I might say, too, that the recent call for a public manifestation by men like Gagnon, Vallières and Chartrand established and escalated the whole coming together of an infiltration of FLQ doctrine in certain areas of society in Quebec – in the unions, among universities and in the media – and the growing feeling among the people of Quebec, particularly the citizens of Montreal, that they are living under a reign of terror. You do not have to ask me; ask any member from Montreal and the people they represent just what they have been undergoing last week in the city of Montreal.
>
> Some hon. Members: Hear, hear!

Mr. Turner (Ottawa-Carleton): I believe we had to respond today in an urgent fashion to the call of the provincial government and the city of Montreal to exercise our duty in a federal state, to ensure that the necessary co-operation in a federal-provincial aspect was maintained between the government of the province of Quebec and the government of Canada. The attorney general of the province of Quebec and the premier of the province of Quebec advised us that the law as presently constituted and directed in a free society was not equipped at the moment to meet the serious situation they were facing, and that they needed additional powers of arrest, of search and of detention.

... This left only two possible courses of action. The government could have sought special legislation of the type embodied in the regulations which have been brought into force under the War Measures or, alternatively, the War Measures Act could have been resorted to.

I suggest to the House that if a special piece of legislation had been resorted to, the provisions might well have been similar to the provisions now found in the regulations. But this government was assured by the government of Quebec, and by senior persons directly involved with attempting to cope with the terrorists, that a search and arrest operation of considerable magnitude directed at the FLQ was necessary and that time was of the essence.

Our initial reaction was the reaction of several members of the House, to seek the authority of Parliament first. But faced with the seriousness of the situation and with the necessity of not broadcasting what the government of Quebec and the government of Canada intended to do, faced with the urgency of anticipating any further escalation in the situation in Montreal, the government of Canada resorted to the War Measures Act. It is my hope that some day the full details of the intelligence upon which the government acted can be made public, because until that day comes the people of Canada will not be able fully to appraise the course of action which has been taken by the government.

The element of surprise was essential, and members of the House will have to rely upon the judgment of the government ...

At a press conference that afternoon Mr Bourassa took complete responsibility for the decision. The danger, he declared, lay in the continued escalation of what was seen as a co-ordinated plan for revolution. Referring to Mr Saulnier's testimony in November 1969 about the activities of the Company of Young Canadians, he said that "continued escalation had revealed the gravity of the situation. First there were violent demonstrations, then there were bombs and afterwards spectacular kidnappings. Obviously this was all of a plan. Logically the fourth stage would be more important still. Action was required because there was no justification for letting this escalation go on and which followed a plan we knew about ... And they even made threats of selected assassinations as part of the fourth stage." As a result, "as soon as the risks of anarchy seemed to acquire a new dimension, I decided to act – firmly and quickly." That night Prime Minister Trudeau made a moving appeal to the nation for understanding and support. "Who are these men who are held out as latter-day patriots and martyrs?" he asked. "Let me describe them to you."

> Three are convicted murderers; five others were jailed for manslaughter; one is serving a life imprisonment after having pleaded guilty to numerous charges related to bombings; another has been convicted of 17 armed robberies; two were once parolled but are now back in jail awaiting trial on charges of robberies.
>
> Yet we are being asked to believe that these persons have been unjustly dealt with, that they have been imprisoned as a result of their political opinions, and that they deserve to be freed immediately, without recourse to due process of law.
>
> The responsibility of deciding whether to release one or another of these criminals is that of the federal government. It is a responsibility that the government will discharge according to law.
>
> To bow to the pressures of these kidnappers who demand that the prisoners be released would be not only an abdication of responsibility, it would lead to an increase in terrorist activities in Quebec.
>
> It would be as well an invitation to terrorism and kidnapping across the country. We might well find ourselves facing an endless series of demands for the release of criminals from jails, from coast to coast, and we would find that the hostages could be innocent members of your family or of your neighborhood.

The federal government was reluctant to use the War Measures Act, he declared, but "following an analysis of the facts, including requests of the government of Quebec and the city of Montreal," decided to proclaim it.

> These are strong powers and I find them as distasteful as I am sure you do. They are necessary, however, to permit the police to deal with persons who advocate or promote the violent overthrow of our democratic system.
>
> In short, I assure you that the government recognizes its grave responsibilities in interfering in certain cases with civil liberties, and that it remains answerable to the people of Canada for its actions.
>
> The government will revoke this proclamation as soon as possible.

The government was not acting "out of fear. It is acting to prevent fear from spreading ... It is acting to make clear to kidnappers, revolutionaries and assassins that in this country laws are made and changed by the elected representatives of all Canadians not by a handful of self-styled dictators. Those who gain power through terror, rule by terror."

The Public Reacts

Public reaction on October 16 and 17 to the use of the War Measures Act and the arrests in Montreal and throughout Quebec was almost predictable. A Canadian Institute of Public Affairs poll on Saturday revealed that 37 per cent of Canadians believed the government was not "tough enough" and 51 per cent felt policy was "about right." The corresponding figures for Quebec alone were 32 per cent and 54 per cent. Outside Quebec, John Robarts informed the Ontario Legislature that he supported Mr Trudeau, and J. C. McRuer, a civil rights trailblazer, declared that the Prime Minister "has done the only thing a responsible man could do in the light of such serious matters which have occurred." In Toronto on October 16 Paul Copeland and Clayton Ruby, two young radical lawyers, called for a mass rally at the City Hall to denounce the "gross overreaction" and the Trudeau "police state." From a much deeper knowledge of Quebec and of civil liberties, Frank Scott replied that "if they use the powers carefully and without abuse – which I think they intend to do – I do not think we have to fear what they do to civil liberties as greatly as that threatened by the FLQ."

The English-Canadian press gave a cautious approval to the act. Most editorial writers were concerned about the suspension of civil liberties, in particular the retroactive clause in the regulations, and most believed that the onus was squarely placed on the government to reveal further justification for the alleged state of "apprehended insurrection." The Toronto *Telegram* (October 16) saw it as "a drastic but necessary action" and the *Winnipeg Free Press* (October 17) as a "desperate cure," an unhappy choice "between anarchy and a period of repressive government ..." The Montreal *Gazette* (October 17) concluded that "it is the only course to take, however distasteful it may appear, if society is to be freed of the threat of continuing terrorism." The *Ottawa Citizen* (October 17) decided that if the nation stood on the brink of civil war then "we give the government full support ... The cause is nothing less than making sure that the people we have elected by democratic process will run this country, and that a band of anonymous criminals will not ... If, however, it is not true ... then woe betide the government that swept freedom away in the name of freedom." The *Globe and Mail* (October 17) agreed: "Only if we can believe that the Government has evidence that the FLQ is strong enough and sufficiently armed to escalate the violence that it has spawned for seven years now, only if we can believe that it is virulent enough to infect other areas of society, only then can the Government's assumption of incredible powers be tolerated." The Vancouver *Province* (October 17) observed how "ill-equipped an open society is to defend itself against disciplined and single-minded force. So with extraordinary political courage, Prime Minister Trudeau has rejected what he calls the bleeding hearts and imposed the War Measures Act. If the choice is, as he suggests, between a society torn by bloody violence or one in which cherished rights are briefly suspended, he will receive overwhelming support."

The *Toronto Star* (October 17) believed that Trudeau "probably had little choice. But he ought to have consulted Parliament before doing so." But the *Star* saw a sinister motive behind Mr Trudeau's decision, however, as did the ultra-nationalists and the left in Quebec. "With such a massive suspension of our civil liberties," wrote a *Star* editor, "the government arouses the suspicion that it is using the War Measures Act not only to crush terrorists but to destroy Quebec nationalism itself and to get such leftists as Stanley Gray – one of the first people arrested – conveniently out of the way." The Vancouver *Sun* (October 16) applauded the decision to "fight fire with fire and match ruthlessness with ruthlessness," while the Saint John *Telegraph-Journal* (October 16) said that "Canada was patient long enough – too long, many of her citizens thought."

Most newspapers seemed to feel that the War Measures Act would deal a fatal blow to the FLQ, if not to the causes of social and economic discontent in Quebec. But the *Brandon Sun* (quoted in the *Telegram*, October 17) expressed the concern of many outside the press that "the government may have struck a great blow for the FLQ. Not at them." The roundup of hundreds of Québécois on the suspicion of being members

A man for all seasons

Ottawa Citizen, November 2, 1970

of or sympathetic to the FLQ, said the *Sun*, would greatly enlarge the forces of radicalism and separatism.

In French Canada *Le Soleil* and *La Presse* supported the use of the act. But Claude Ryan (*Le Devoir*, October 17) did not, and saw only that Mr Bourassa had finally yielded to Mr Trudeau and that Quebec had been taken over by Ottawa:

... Forgetting any slight misgivings which he might have felt in this respect, Mr Bourassa has, in the final analysis, opted for calling on the powers in Ottawa. In requesting the enforcement of the War Measures Act on his own initiative the Prime Minister of Quebec was in fact concurring in the subordination of his government to that of Mr Trudeau. In the eyes of the rest of the country he confirmed what had been a memory from the past – that Ottawa is the seat of real national government and that Quebec is after all only a rather more troublesome province than the others.

This sudden switch is contrary to developments during the past ten years. It may be an indication of what might happen in other areas. At the heart of a crisis Mr Bourassa has given way once to fear. He may find it difficult to cast off the impression he has given, be it in the eyes of his federal colleagues or in those of his own fellow citizens.

As for Mr Trudeau, he may for the time being manage to crush the FLQ. But he will not be able to stop some ideas from flourishing and maybe even, with Ottawa's help, spreading. He should not forget that as far as the present crisis is concerned "the final question" has only been set aside and ultimately it will have to be settled in Quebec itself, without outside interference. The man who formerly preached mistrust of the establishment has today become a military protector. It would be a vain task to search in texts bearing his signature traces of such qualities as rationalisation, free consent, restraint or respect based on equality, which he formerly took pleasure in identifying with federalism. Mr Trudeau may say that he was forced to make his choice; the reply of many may be that he deserved it ...

Mr Ryan's assessment was very close to that of René Lévesque, who bluntly declared that Quebec was without a government. In a lengthy statement on Friday night, Lévesque declared:

... Quebec no longer has a government.

The bit of country over which we had any control has been swept away by the first hard blow. The Bourassa cabinet has stepped down and is no more than a puppet in the hands of the federal leaders.

It is now quite obvious that – right from the beginning of this tragic period which began with Mr Cross' kidnapping – the only part played by the government has been as walk-on. We are unfortunately forced to believe that even while the pseudo-negotiations opened last Sunday by Mr Bourassa were going on he was, according to an agreement, merely acting as the tool of a policy which had been formulated without referring to him, and that he adopted a compromising attitude while knowing all the time about the rigid line which Ottawa had chosen; that in fact he had been preparing the necessary climate, meanwhile letting the situation continue and deteriorate while pretending to hesitate, and that, finally, last night, it was he who sanctioned the extreme steps taken by the Trudeau régime, whereby all of Quebec is put under military occupation until next spring.

... Nor can we help thinking and saying that this degradation of Quebec was intended – quite consciously by some and instinctively by others.

The guiding factors have taken two extreme forms.

Firstly there is the thoroughly official, legally recognized federal establishment, backed by economic and other forces. It was from here that the first murmur was heard of the likelihood of resorting to all means including military force for the purpose of keeping Quebec, and, if need be, putting it in its place.

For years it has been in this area that attempts have been made to stifle the hopes of the Québécois, howsoever moderately ambitious they might have been, swamping them in the undergrowth of committees, meetings, and eternal new beginnings. We are obliged to say that from the highest levels of this establishment orders were given for that non-stop flow of propaganda the aim of which was disfigure and ridicule every aspect of democratic nationalism in Quebec at all costs, and which knew no bounds, resorting to the worst type of slander in order to prove subversion and terrorism.

At the other extreme let us hope that those very people who threw themselves body and soul into a career of subversion and terrorism – both of which are so tragically contrary to the best interests of our people – may at least realize now that they have in fact been the forerunners of the military régime thereby endangering the basic rights of all Québécois.

Finally, we do not know how large the revolutionary army is or was, nor the extent of their power to create disorder and anarchy. Until we receive proof to the contrary – and every responsible citizen should demand this proof and be given it as soon as possible if it exists or else drop out from a self-respecting society – until we receive proof to the contrary we will believe that such a minute, numerically unimportant fraction is involved, that rushing into the enforcement of the War Measures Act was a panicky and altogether excessive reaction, especially when you think of the inordinate length of time they want to maintain this régime.

The most worrying thing – and this might also reveal quite specific and even more inadmissible intentions, is that the arrests, the detentions (whether preventive or otherwise) and the searches, have taken on the proportions of a full police operation right across Quebec.

We believe that in this respect at least (which is the most urgent) we can call on all Québécois, especially those who are highly placed, fully confident that at this time of such unprecedented gravity we will find enough solidarity and calm democratic strength to prevent this dangerous climate from degenerating into blind repression ...

In view of the extremes which have for all practical purposes caused the destruction of our government, Quebec's democrats must overcome their differences of opinion immediately and find the means or the organizations for building the moral power necessary to defend our basic liberties and, at the same time, all our hopes for the future ...

Early Saturday morning the leaders of the Quebec labour movement issued a statement condemning "the régime of force imposed by the Trudeau government":

Following an extraordinary meeting Friday night, October 16, at Quebec City, the executives of the three parent labour bodies – the CNTU, QFL, and CEQ – denounced the attitude of the Bourassa government which, without an apparent and justifiable reason, moved overnight from a position which appeared to us to have been carefully considered to an inexplicable attitude of total submission to federal power.

The parent bodies had endorsed a position taken by a group of Quebec citizens, including the officers of the three bodies, supporting the intention of the Bourassa government to negotiate an exchange of FLQ hostages and political prisoners. But without any explanation or apparent reason, the Bourassa government ended the negotiations and implored the federal government to place Quebec under military rule.

The three parent bodies must denounce the régime of force imposed by the Trudeau government, alerted by the surrender of the Bourassa government which panicked, impinging on the civil responsibilities of Quebec citizens and setting up a sort of rigid military régime, such as can be found in a banana republic where military juntas are lord and master.

As representatives of parent unions and also as citizens of Quebec, we deplore what seems to us to be a plot between the governments of Quebec and Ottawa to make the rest of the country and the world believe that anarchy reigns in Quebec, that there is chaos and insurrection while in fact the citizens of Quebec are beginning to show that a democracy is viable in Quebec.

The union movements are consternated by the suppression of civil liberties which threaten democracy more than they threaten terrorism, while the two governments know very well that there are more social ills to correct than there is anarchy to repress. We equally deplore the radical method employed by the FLQ and ask, as evidence of their good faith, that the hostages be released.

Faced with the urgency of the situation, the executives of the three parent unions, have decided to call an extraordinary plenary session, the supreme authority of their organizations between conventions, in order to decide the methods of action to be taken to save democracy in Quebec. This meeting has been fixed for October 21, at 2 PM in Quebec.

The editors of *Québec-Presse* (October 18) went further and called for passive resistance:

Repression is on the move. Political repression ...

... Jean Marchand, federal minister, has made a public declaration that the government was amazed that the people of Quebec did not unanimously condemn with all their strength the FLQ's action. The attitude adopted by Quebec and the Québécois shook the government in Ottawa and made them afraid.

It therefore became necessary to take severe measures against the obvious approval which part of the population had given to the FLQ manifesto. Firm action would have to be taken. Whence the War Measures and the arrival of the army. Whence the clearly political repression.

Second stage in the operation: brainwashing.

The operation was set in motion in Ottawa. Pierre Elliott Trudeau opened fire. On Friday evening he spoke on radio and television. He was frightening and this is what he wanted to be. In fact, he was terrifying, in more than one respect. After the violence of weapons and soldiers that of untruths was coming onto the scene ...

... Now this is quite clear, the FLQ's target is not just any part of the population. As it has said itself, its target is the representatives of the forces in control of Quebec. This is quite another matter.

For proof one only has to see where the military have been posted in the Montreal area. There are very few in the Francophone eastern section and there are very many in Westmount.

It is the owner minority which must be protected.

The army is not in Quebec to protect the population. It is in Quebec to protect the owners. And as everyone knows Trudeau and Bourassa are at the top of the list.

Consequently we must resist the repression which is striking everywhere in Quebec. And we must do so by all possible peaceful means. We therefore agree with those citizens who, in our "viewpoint" page, call for passive resistance. It is up to popular movements, citizens committees, all associations, and above all the unions to organize this resistance in a common, concerted effort.

"This cruel and senseless act"

OCTOBER 17–20

NOTHING had been heard from the FLQ cells since the morning of October 14. But at 10 AM October 17 the Liberation cell penned its tenth communiqué. Receipt of the communiqué was not made public, however, until Mr Choquette read it in the National Assembly on December 8:

The present authorities have declared war on the Quebec patriots. After having pretended to negotiate for several days they have finally revealed their true face as hypocrites and terrorists.

The colonial army has come to give assistance to the "bouncers" of Drapeau the "dog." Their objective: to terrorize the population by massive and illegal arrests and searches, by large and noisy deployments, and by making shattering statements on the urgent situation in Quebec, etc.

They must, at all costs, undermine the dangerous sympathy that a large number of Québécois feel towards the patriots of the Front de libération du Québec since the kidnapping of J. Cross and Pierre Laporte, and since the publication of the manifesto of the Front de libération du Québec. Consequently, the Front de libération du Québec declares:

1 The death sentence against J. Cross is suspended indefinitely. J. Cross remains a prisoner of the Front de libération du Québec and will not be released until the present authorities have complied with our demands. He will only be executed if it should occur that the fascist police discover us and attempt to intervene.

2 As for Pierre Laporte, the Chenier cell of the Front de libération du Québec is presently studying his case and will makes its decision known shortly.

3 We ask that all the action cells of the Front de libération du Québec, as well as all determined Québécois, go into action in an attempt to undermine the decisions of the fascist authorities so that the patriot political prisoners will be released.

We shall overcome. The Front de libération du Québec.

Following are two remarks: 1 We thank Mr Robert Lemieux for his devotion to duty which, fortunately or otherwise, served only to reveal the hypocrisy of the fascist authorities. 2 We are attaching a personal letter from J. Cross to his wife to this communiqué.

(Bernard Mergler, the lawyer who negotiated the release of James Cross, later said that Jacques Lanctôt, one of the kidnappers, told him that "we felt that this communiqué would serve as an example and a direction to the Chenier cell and that they would follow our lead. But the police concealed it.")

The telephone at CKAC rang at seven o'clock on the night of October 17 and reporter Norman Maltais was told that the body of Pierre Laporte could be found in an abandoned car near the St Hubert airfield. Reporters, like the police, were wearied by anonymous calls, and Maltais did nothing. "I started wondering only when the same person called again and asked why we had not announced Laporte's execution on the air," he said later. Mr Maltais explained that the station could not publicize or follow up every anonymous call, and the voice replied that he would call later. At 9:30 he telephoned to say that there was a communication at the Place des Arts. Maltais sent Michel Saint-Louis to the Place des Arts, where he found the following communiqué:

In face of the arrogance of the federal government and its lackey Bourassa, in the face of their obvious bad faith, the FLQ has therefore decided to act.

Pierre Laporte, minister of unemployment and assimilation, has been executed at 6:18 tonight by the Dieppe cell (Royal 22nd). You will find the body in the trunk of the green Chevrolet (9J-2420) at the St Hubert base, entry no 2.

We shall overcome.

FLQ

P.S. The exploiters of the Quebec people had better watch out.

Michel Saint-Louis located the car and called the police.

As the police and the army gathered their demolition squads, Prime Minister Bourassa, apparently unaware of the unfolding tragedy at St Hubert, issued another statement to the kidnappers at 11:30:

Quebec, October 17, 1970

The serious measures taken by the Quebec government have brought about the calm necessary for decisive action. The authorities are therefore informing the abductors of Mr Cross and Mr Laporte of the following details of the final offer which was formulated by these same authorities. These details specify the technicalities of their offer to the abductors, which should permit the attaining of the desired objective, namely the safe return of Mr Cross and Mr Laporte in the nicest possible way.

The population understands that unprecedented security measures have been brought into force. However, we recommend that everyone attend to his usual occupations; in this way, the population has no reason to feel uneasy, especially if no one approaches the areas mentioned further on.

The authorities are relying on the co-operation of everyone; this will be the best way for each one of us to help in the saving of these human lives.

Here are the essential details with regard to the previous question and to the offer of the Quebec government. These details are communicated by lawyer Robert Demers, representing the authorities concerned. They constitute the modalities for the release of the hostages and the safe conduct of the abductors. It is at the request of the Canadian government, made for humanitarian reasons, that the Cuban government consented, for these same reasons, to authorize its representative to participate in these modalities.

A – The abductors, still carrying their weapons, and accompanied by Mr Laporte, must go by way of the Concorde Bridge to Man and His World, the area designated in agreement with the Canadian and Cuban governments as being an extension of the Cuban Consulate in Montreal. This extension covers all the privileges and immunities accorded to a consulate.

B – The route leading to the designated area will be completely cleared or guarded by the police and the army. To have this done the abductors will simply have to ask by calling the Sûreté du Québec at 395–4195. The military and the police will then receive the order to let the abductors, still carrying their weapons, to pass uninjured, driving to the designated area, accompanied by Mr Cross and Mr Laporte.

C – Upon their arrival at the designated area, the abductors will deliver Mr Cross and Mr Laporte to the Cuban government represented by its Consul. The Cuban Consul will then ask the abductors to hand over their arms.

D – Within the hour following their arrival at the designated area, the abductors, accompanied by the Cuban Consul, will be driven to the airport where they will board a plane. A limited number of Canadian officials and representatives of the Cuban government will accompany the abductors.

F – Travel documents will be prepared and given to the passengers.

G – The Canadian government has arrived at an agreement with the Cuban government on this plan in conjunction with the government of Quebec.

As Mr Bourassa was speaking the demolition squad carefully approached the car. From behind a metal shield the men pried at the trunk, until at 12:25 AM October 18 it opened. The crumpled and bloody body was identified as that of Pierre Laporte. In Ottawa the House was still in session, although most members were watching the drama on television not listening to Robert Borrie on the War Measures Act. At 12:50 Mr Borrie was informed that Mr Laporte's body had been identified. "I think that this news firmly entrenches my opinion, views and conviction that this government has acted in a proper way," he said. "We are not dealing with political dissenters; we are dealing with organized murderers." Although an adjournment was clearly called for, Stanley Knowles took the floor to argue that "in our kind of society we still think there is a better way than to use force or repression to deal with ideas we do not like." Marcel Prud'homme cried "Enough," but Mr Knowles continued until Mr Prud'homme rose on a question of privilege to suggest that "under the circumstances the best thing the hon. member could do would be to offer his silence for a better united Canada." Mr Knowles finally relented, and the Commons adjourned at 1:05.

By then several hundred people had gathered on the Hill, numbed and

The shot that unified a nation

Chronicle-Herald, Halifax, October 19, 1970

silent, or whispering in small knots. There was polite applause as the Prime Minister reached the Hill, and strode, white-faced, to Jean Marchand's office. For some time they waited for further word from Montreal, where there were rumours that a second body had been located. By 3 AM the rumours had been scotched, and Mr Trudeau spoke briefly to the nation on television:

It is with shock and consternation I believe that all Canadians have learned of the death of Mr. Pierre Laporte, who was so cowardly assassinated by a band of murderers and I can't help feeling as a Canadian, a deep sense of shame that this cruel and senseless act should have been conceived in cold blood and executed in like manner.

I want to express to Mrs. Laporte and Mr. Laporte's family the very deep regret of the Canadian people and of the Canadian government and our desire as Canadians to stick together in this very sorry moment of our history.

On Sunday Montreal police continued their searches and arrests, and issued an all-points bulletin for Paul Rose and Marc Carbonneau, the prime suspects in the two kidnappings. The Prime Minister held an early cabinet meeting before meeting Bourassa and Drapeau in Montreal and visiting the Courthouse where Mr Laporte's body lay. Meanwhile, through CKLM, a letter from Mr Cross (who had heard his death announced on television the night before) was found in a church in east end Montreal:

To the government authorities:

I wish to reassure all involved that I am alive and well and in good health. My life is not in danger for the time being. The FLQ which kidnapped me told me that I was a political prisoner and that I would remain as such so long as the authorities refused to release the political prisoners presently in jail in Quebec.

The only danger to my life would be if police discovered the place where I am being held and tried to interfere.

The FLQ will not give up and I shall be the first to die.

Early this morning I noticed that my death was being reported on television. It was terrible. I wrote a letter to my wife yesterday. It was dated yesterday morning, but the word "morning" was erased. It was placed in the hall of the Church of St Jean Baptiste de la Salle, 2585 Boulevard Pie IX, and the stations CKLM and CKAC were advised, but nobody went there.

Despite this letter, my death has been announced along with the fact that my body has been discovered. This must have been terrifying for my wife.

The FLQ states that it would be better for all concerned if the government releases the political prisoners as requested.

The authorities will never find the place where I am being detained.

I am a prisoner in the same way that members of the FLQ are presently prisoners.

Perhaps the Red Cross or the Cuban consulate could act as intermediaries, my exchange for the release of the FLQ prisoners.

All this can be done without violence, and I hope that this will be believed. I am sending a separate letter to my wife.

J. R. Cross

At four in the afternoon Mr Bourassa spoke on television, promising that "the government of which I am the leader will not allow itself to go under because of such an experience. It will face up with all the determination needed. I am convinced that Pierre Laporte would have had this will to overcome." At eleven the Prime Minister appeared on both the English and French network. In English he described the FLQ as "members of a hard core devoted to a single purpose – to inspire within all of us fear and hatred and in this atmosphere to destroy our nation. They are beneath contempt." Pierre Laporte was a man "who had devoted his life to the betterment of the people of Quebec ... His record of struggle and accomplishment sounds out like a trumpet in comparison to the whines of self-pity and the screams of hatred which have poured forth from the FLQ. Yet this was the man the FLQ murdered in cold blood." The FLQ, he promised, "has sown the seeds of its own destruction. It has revealed that it has no mandate but terror, no policies but violence, and no solutions but murder. Savagery is alien to Canadians, it always will be, for collectively we will not tolerate it." To French Canadians he declared:

> ... Imbued with hate the FLQ has turned to violence to stir up hate, to keep it going and to spread it in this insidious fashion, hoping thereby that disorder, upset, and panic will become generalized. That is its primary aim. That is the trap laid for us; to divide us one from the other, to split us up through hate and racism, to make disagreements between generations so bad as to be beyond solution. Therefore, if the terrorists are provoking us in so many ways, they do so to bring about as much discord as possible and to create a climate to suit their own ambitions. Since they are incapable of winning in a free world, they would like to win in a state of tyranny. Do not let us fall into their trap. All those who hold responsible positions in any area of our society must think ahead objectively. In such tragic circumstances it is vital not to take advantage of the situation in order to encourage bitterness or animosity. In so doing we would waste the energy needed for devoting to the betterment of our society. These loveless creatures who have tried to divide us through tragedy, have today caused us to unite together in a common purpose. At this time the only strong feelings we should have should be a desire for justice. With the help of justice we shall defend our values, our order, our laws. With its help we shall rediscover our peace and freedom.

The newspapers of October 19 left no doubt where most Canadians stood. "The crime is treason, the punishment hanging," headlined a *Province* editorial. The *Globe and Mail* warned the government not to move another inch in negotiating with the murderers. Many English-Canadian newspapers turned their anger on those who had spoken out against the War Measures Act. The Halifax *Chronicle-Herald* wrote that "the loud protestations of misguided people, in Quebec and elsewhere in Canada, about the loss of 'democratic rights' ... have a mocking ring in the aftermath of Mr Laporte's murder. Since organizations, like people, are judged by their actions, those who, after this weekend's diabolical happenings, continue to voice outright support for the FLQ must reasonably be assumed to approve of murder as a political weapon." Bruce West, that mirror of traditional English-Canadian society, warned that "those who have taken to the streets and the public squares with their bullhorns to attack the courageous stand of the Canadian Government in this grave hour should be plainly informed that the vast majority of our people are no longer in a mood to indulge in long and academic arguments about possible threats to our civil liberties" (*Globe and Mail*, October 19). In urging the debating society on Parliament Hill to approve the War Measures Act at once, Mr West was joined by the Toronto *Telegram* which ordered all MPs to vote immediately for the measure. The MPs hardly needed to be told, as the mail to Ottawa was overwhelmingly in favour of

Winnipeg Free Press, October 20, 1970

the government, and they voted 190 to 16. Four members of the NDP – Howard, Saltsman, Winch, and Mather – broke party ranks to support the government.

In Quebec Réal Caouette urged that the FLQ members in custody be placed before a firing squad, but Père Vincent Harvey, the separatist Dominican who edited *Maintenant*, declared that "It is too easy to say that Pierre Laporte was killed by a handful of terrorists. A handful of terrorists with their finger on the trigger. But who put the gun into their hands? ... I refuse to pass judgment" (*Québec-Presse*, October 25). Claude Ryan was prepared to judge, however, and condemned an assassination executed with "a cold-bloodedness which arouses horror and repulsion." Admitting that he found the War Measures Act excessive, Mr Ryan no longer seemed to doubt the need for exceptional measures but urged that they be applied "with a maximum of discretion": for, he argued, "The exclusive use of protective devices and manhunts will not solve much, however, over a long-term period. For one citizen found guilty of crime there is a risk that two, three, five citizens will be outraged at the abuse to their rights, if the powers of discretion are misused. Unless we are careful this might encourage a climate of exasperation not unlike the growth of a phenomenon like the FLQ." And once again he returned to his sermon about the fragility of Quebec's political leadership:

Whether we like it or not the dark hours through which Quebec is passing are raising doubts about the political régime and economic and social structures under which we have lived for a century. Such serious – and such widespread – ills do not come about spontaneously; they grow in the proper soil. During this crisis it is more important than ever before that citizens give their wholehearted support to rational decisions made by their legitimate political leaders, and even that, when full explanations cannot be given forthwith, they allow these leaders the benefit of the doubt. But it is equally important that the political leaders abandon their complacency and humbly face up to the tenuousness of their leadership which they should work at consolidating by involving to a greater extent all those – from all walks of life – whose social influence and moral authority take another form – no less vital but often overlooked by political powers – of democratic leadership. Our immediate aim is not to save the prestige or authority of this person or that, but to save democracy in Quebec. This is the aim to which we must cling throughout the unprecedented gloom of this night through which Quebec is passing.

In *La Presse* both Jean-Paul Desbiens and Jean Pellerin wrote major editorials. To Pellerin the issue was straightforward: "for the humble citizen the time has come to choose between the FLQ and the government. The time has come for each of us to ask himself which is better: to allow the FLQ to continue harming civil rights, or to let the government put a temporary stop to its pleasure?" Desbiens echoed the same sentiments:

This is not the time to split hairs. As of today the people must declare their support of the government in every way possible ... No citizen should hold back from the government, for government is all of us. And only governmental apparatus can free liberty. Otherwise each citizen would have to fend for himself ...

This is not the time to listen to the intellectuals who are talking about the sex of liberty and who are arousing children. There again, they are not a majority. And there too responsible intellectuals must pull themselves together.

Questioned by journalists Paul Cliche did not hesitate to deplore Laporte's murder. His comment led to a motion of censure by the permanent council against him and two FRAP candidates, Emile Boudreau and Michel Cartier, who had also condemned the violence of the FLQ, for deviating from the policy established by FRAP on October 11.

Letters and telegrams in support of the government flooded Ottawa. A public opinion survey, released on CTV's "W5" on November 15, revealed that 87 per cent approved of the use of the War Measures Act, and less than 6 per cent disapproved of Mr Trudeau's actions during the crisis. (The survey also revealed that more than 50 per cent of those polled

Toronto Daily Star, October 27, 1970

favoured the prevention or suppression of communist demonstrations and student militants, 43 per cent hippies, and more than 30 per cent labour militants and womens lib.) The intensity of popular feeling was frightening. In Acton Vale in Bagot County residents were shocked when a few young people gathered in the tavern on Sunday night "to celebrate the death of Pierre Laporte and toast the FLQ." Said Mayor Henri Boisvert: "These are the sort of people this law is aimed at and they are the ones who are going to get it." From Nicolet, former Tory MP and UN cabinet minister Clement Vincent reported that "People here are remaining calm – but there's a dangerous force underneath. Some are on the verge of taking vengeance into their own hands." Out in British Columbia, on October 22 the cabinet issued an order-in-council stating that "no person teaching or instructing our youth in an educational institution receiving Government support shall be in the employment of that institution if he or she advocates the policies of the FLQ or the overthrow of democratically elected governments by violent means." In Dawson Creek the school board fired a teacher, Arthur Olsen, apparently for suggesting that there was no difference between the Russian invasion of Czechoslovakia and the occupation of Quebec.

Opposition to the War Measures Act remained alive, however. The NDP saw four men break ranks but the party leadership steadfastly remained critical. In Montreal the central council of the Montreal CNTU declared on October 20 that "Quebec will never emerge from this state of perpetual crisis except by accession to political sovereignty and the implementation of a society where wage earners are in power." And a day later, the three senior labour organizations – the CNTU, Quebec Federation of Labour, and the Quebec Teachers Corporation – met again to demand the withdrawal of the War Measures Act and negotiations for the release of Mr Cross. While the unions condemned the "criminal acts" of the FLQ, a summary statement of their position displayed prominently in *Le Travail* said that in supporting those who wished to safeguard the status quo the government had really taken the life of Pierre Laporte:

Would
YOU
with good conscience, have taken the decision to let Pierre Laporte be murdered?

Is there anyone in your family or amongst your friends who would have taken the decision to let Pierre Laporte be murdered?
Probably
NOT

Well, out of the 700 active unionists who attended the extraordinary meeting of the three senior labour organizations on Wednesday, October 21, in Quebec, there wasn't anyone who would have taken the decision to let Pierre Laporte be murdered.

That's one reason to explain the position adopted by the three senior labour organizations.

So long as the government of Quebec showed that it sincerely wanted to negotiate with the FLQ to save the lives of Pierre Laporte and the diplomat James Cross, the union movement
WAS IN AGREEMENT
with this attitude.

But as soon as the government of Quebec gave in to pressure from Ottawa and adopted an unyielding attitude, thereby endangering the lives of Pierre Laporte and James Cross, from then on the union movement appealed to good sense:

The union movement told the government that
IT DID NOT HAVE THE RIGHT
to take such a risk.

If the government took such a risk, it is because someone somewhere decided that, whatsoever the consequences, they would let Pierre Laporte and James Cross be murdered.

Such a decision would never have been taken by the union leaders, nor by any normal citizen.

Someone someplace made a choice between the lives of two men and something else.

What was the other choice?

It is a social, economic, and political régime that the union movement is working to change, because it is a régime that tolerates too much injustice.

This régime – which the union movement is trying to change for the better – would retain its status quo if some members of our society had their way.

Others are prepared to defend this régime even at the cost of a military occupation, even at the cost of illegal imprisonment of many of our citizens, even at the cost of human life.

The government has made a choice.

It has taken the side of those who want the régime to continue unchanged.

This choice has already cost Pierre Laporte his life.

THE UNION MOVEMENT HAS CHOSEN BETWEEN HUMAN LIFE AND WHAT THE GOVERNMENT CALLS REASONS OF STATE – IT HAS OPTED FOR HUMAN LIFE, WITH ALL THE CONSEQUENCES SUCH A CHOICE MAY INVOLVE.

But within twenty-four hours, according to Pierre Vennat (*La Presse*, October 23), it was clear that the central councils were not carrying their membership.

The Montreal Election

OCTOBER 21–26

MEANWHILE, the government remained under pressure to provide fuller details on the apprehended insurrection feared by Mr Bourassa and Mr Drapeau. Outside the House on October 21 Jean Marchand presented his views to Jack Webster, host of a hot-line show for CKNW in Vancouver. "What can you tell my west coast listeners what it means, apprehended insurrection. What are your fears?" asked Webster.

MARCHAND – Well first, I understand that they don't understand exactly what is going on in Quebec because if there were 25 or 50,000 FLQ members in Quebec well everybody would be aware. But they are not so many. The problem is that they have had the training very important to insurrection and they have some sympathy outside. What if they had some front organization? (pause) and at this moment in Montreal as you know there is an election. There is no relation in our action to the election itself but we had good reason to believe that the FLQ which (pause) as a front has the organization called FRAP [le Front d'action politique] in Montreal and is running candidates in Montreal, wanted to disturb the election by explosions of all kinds and by further kidnappings or even shooting (pause) people. So we found it was very dangerous. It was not only a case of two kidnappings, though this was important in itself, our action couldn't be explained only by this. We knew something about this background and this is why we thought it was important to act and it was important because the province of Quebec asked us to act and the City of Montreal, too. And I don't know if what we were afraid of would have happened anyhow. I don't know. We'll never know. But if it had happened, knowing what we knew and we hadn't done anything of course nobody would have understood. You knew all these things. You had the requests from Quebec, from Montreal and you knew all what you are saying now and you didn't do anything. Of course the government of Canada would have blown up.

WEBSTER – You have the FLQ. We are naming the FLQ as you have done as the outlawed activist, terrorist organization. Correct. Can you tell me what, have you any idea of the strength or the size, and I want you to tell me about the arms and ammunition of the FLQ.

MARCHAND – This we don't know exactly. We know there are about two tons of dynamite that have been stolen in Quebec. Where are those two tons, I don't know, but presumably they are in control of them. There are more

Halloween fantasy?

Ottawa Citizen, October 23, 1970

than 100 rifles that have been stolen from a ship, a Japanese ship, in Montreal and other guns which have been stolen elsewhere. So how much arms they have we don't know but we know very well that they have enough dynamite to blow up the heart of Montreal.

WEBSTER – You must have had enough information to implement the almost totalitarian War Measures Act.

MARCHAND – Of course we would have preferred to have another act to intervene in that case because I think that the War Measures Act is not in proportion even with the problem as I have described it, but we had no other means.

WEBSTER – The FLQ though, I have not been able anywhere to get an impression of its size. Is it 30 men, is it 300 men, or they've got 4,500 weapons, I'm told, is it 4,000?

MARCHAND – Well, I don't know. It might be something between 1,000 and 3,000. Now all members of the FLQ are not terrorists. But there are enough to create a lot of trouble and a lot of killing and this is what we have tried to prevent ... (*Montreal Star*, October 22).

With the Montreal civic election on October 25 Mr Marchand's statement made the headlines: "JEAN MARCHAND : le FRAP est une couverture pour le FLQ" ran *La Presse*'s black line. Contacted by the *Montreal Star* on the night of October 21, Mr Marchand denied that he had equated FRAP and the FLQ. He stated that he suspected some people were members of both, "but I couldn't have said that FRAP and the FLQ are the same thing because I don't believe it. I think FRAP's support of the FLQ manifesto was politically gauche and tactically stupid and I don't understand why they did it." In a tumultuous Commons on October 22 he confessed that he had used the word "front" incorrectly in English, and the association between FRAP and the FLQ was rejected by the Prime Minister.

But Mr Marchand's statement did nothing to explain the background to the apprehended insurrection; on the contrary, it fed the belief among the left that the act had been designed to crush not the FLQ but the nationalist and leftist opposition to the governments in Ottawa, Quebec City, and Montreal. Mayor Drapeau, who had nothing to fear electorally from FRAP, repeatedly drew a connection between his electoral opponents and the FLQ. One interview was on CKAC:

Interviewer: You say there are some affinities between FRAP and the FLQ. Can you elaborate on that? What are those affinities?

Mr Drapeau: First of all, this municipal movement, this para-municipal movement is a collection of everything that is terrorist and revolutionary. For its big rally one week ago Sunday in the St Louis de France Church Hall, its main guest speaker or just about was Michel Chartrand who made incredible statements. Everybody knows that Michel Chartrand is a revolutionary terrorist who advocates the use of violence, bombs, and threats, and who rejoices over kidnappings ...

After the kidnapping of Mr Pierre Laporte, he went in front of the residence of Mr Pierre Laporte in St Lambert to yell insults. At a rally at the Paul Sauvé Arena (last Thursday) he made fun of the kidnapping by saying that people had no cause to worry because the Minister of Unemployment, as he called him, was serving time in the penalty box. We all know about the tragedy that resulted from this so-called penalty, to use the phrase of this revolutionary terrorist. The same movement announced that it had unanimously passed a resolution, and I quote *Le Devoir*, reading, "Taking a stand on the latest actions of the FLQ, FRAP declares that its main objective is the accession of the workers of Quebec to political and economic power and that in this sense, it agrees with the FLQ." The article in *Le Devoir* added the following: "Paul Cliche, the FRAP president, announced this position at a rally attended by one thousand party workers and supporters, after it had been adopted unanimously by the FRAP permanent council, which includes two representatives from each ward organization. FRAP says it is convinced that the FLQ does not want to terrorize the workers, but those who use violence against the workers."

This statement means that they approve of terrorists. So, let us not play on words any longer about this. This is a statement from FRAP. There is more, not just the rally and the statement. For example, we know that Mr Michel Chartrand is quoted in the latest issue of *Time* magazine, dated October 26, as having declared at the Nelson Hotel during the days when Mr Robert Lemieux gave his press conferences and I quote now in English, "Now Chartrand shouted to a newsman across the bar in the Hotel Nelson. 'We are going to win because there are more boys ready to shoot members of Parliament than there are policemen, my friend.' " These are his words, and here is a favourite orator of the para-municipal electoral movement.

And there is more. Last Thursday at the Paul Sauvé Arena there was a rally of this FRAP and what happened? We only have to look at the *Montreal Star* and other newspapers, but I show you now the *Star*, Mr Lévesque, which has a big picture on page three, a big picture showing Michel Chartrand addressing the assembly. The caption underneath reads: "Labor leader addresses the pro-FLQ FRAP rally attended by more than 1,500 students in the Paul Sauvé Arena last night." And all the other papers made the same report. I have here *La Presse*, with a headline across eight columns: "3,000 People Chant FLQ, FLQ, FLQ." And this was happening in the hall rented by FRAP at the Paul Sauvé centre last Thursday, the same day when the Canadian army entered Montreal to protect the public institutions, the telecommunications, and to prevent everything from being blown up.

Interviewer: Excuse me for interrupting, Mayor Drapeau, but I am sure you could speak on this aspect at great length and we have no doubt this is true. However, on this programme yesterday, Mr Cliche said he agreed with certain social objectives of the FLQ, but that he disagreed completely with the use of any violent means.

Mr Drapeau: I will give you an example of what I mean. On October 5, the Civic party held at the Champlain Theatre, the same place where my party was founded, a great rally for mostly all the organizers from the eighteen districts of Montreal to celebrate our tenth anniversary, and on this occasion we made public our programme and we presented our candidates. We addressed about fifteen hundred organizers and supporters of the Civic party.

If that night, the night of Mr Cross's kidnapping, we had invited Pierre Vallières, Charles Gagnon, Robert Lemieux, and Michel Chartrand to talk to our members, would people not have said everywhere that the Civic party had an assistance pact with the FLQ? Of course, it would have been said. That is what it would have meant. So it does not matter what they say on your station, the Montreal public and the people outside Montreal who read the newspapers, who saw the Vallières, the Gagnons, the Lemieux, and the Chartrands, proclaim and promote on television, radio and in newspapers, and in press conferences, the acts of violence. We know these leftovers from prisons, forgive the expression, but it is because people were assassinated that they were in prison and they deserve to be in prison – the Vallières and Gagnons, now out of prison, giving press conferences broadcast by radio and television. The people who are listening now have seen these people. To say that violence is necessary and that the revolution should be continued and that would be their purpose during their freedom on bail, well, when do you see a pact of assistance as open as that? Even if they come and say something nice on CKAC or on Radio-Canada, I do not believe that the citizens of Montreal will be so naïve as to believe it. When one opens the hall at St Louis de France to revolutionaries and terrorists so that they may address their members, I say that the third gesture, if ever the movement took over the administration of the city, would be to open wide the doors of City Hall to the FLQ. And I believe that the entire population must agree with me. One never sees two without three.

The partial text of another interview with Herb Marshall of CFOX on October 22 was published in the *Gazette* two days later:

Mr Drapeau: I don't think that this movement can deny the open sympathy they have for the FLQ. They invited to their hall Vallières, Gagnon, and Chartrand who are admitting they are advocating the revolution ...

Mr Marshall: Was this then the reason you asked for the War Measures Act?

Mr Drapeau: Not at all. This has nothing to do with the War Measures Act. The army was here when the meeting took place. It is because the revolution is in preparation that we asked for help from higher government; we didn't refer to any specific acts.

The revolution was started, this is what people don't believe. I don't know what evidence is needed. It was not only apprehended, it was started.

Mr Marshall: Then would you say there will be blood running in the streets and everything during this cam...

Mr Drapeau: Definitely so, definitely so.

Mr Marshall: How do you mean that?

Mr Drapeau: I don't think we have to hide that the blood of Mr Laporte has already been spilled on the floor of a garage on Armstrong Street and that the blood of Mr Cross is still threatened.

And these are only two cases. I could tell you about the threats that other persons and myself have received and about the plans to blow up public services and telecommunications and the kidnapping of other persons. The plan is there and it is being executed. We are satisfied it is the FLQ ...

Asked on October 23 if he thought an insurrection was planned for October 25, the Mayor replied: "Without the presence of the army and without the very strongest measures taken by the federal government there would have been an insurrection. There would never have been an election" (*Gazette*, October 24).

Paul Cliche, the head of FRAP, denounced the Drapeau-Marchand statements as a manœuvre similar "to the Brinks trucks business" on the eve of the April 29 election. Under the circumstances, said Cliche: "the elections have lost practically all meaning, but the only way the people of Montreal can protest is by voting next Sunday and to this end FRAP is continuing the struggle, in spite of the unfair repression to which it is being subjected, in spite of the psychological and moral terrorism being practised by Messrs Marchand and Drapeau, in spite of intimidation and harassment to which its workers are being exposed during their campaign (searches, people going from door to door being followed by police in cars)." It was his opponents, argued Cliche, who appealed to violence: "If we had made a statement ten times less violent and libellous than the ones made by them, we would already be behind bars." Repeating that their aim was to secure working class power by democratic means, Cliche warned that the election would not be the end and that "FRAP reckons that it is the salaried workers who will decide for FRAP what methods and actions should be followed after October 25, and not the Marchands, Trudeaus, and company with the federal army." (At the same press conference Mr Cliche later said that he had again denounced the violence of the FLQ, "but the Anglophone spokesman ... Dr Howard Bergman, of the St James CAP, formally contradicted me a few minutes later by saying that FRAP had never condemned the FLQ.") FRAP also filed a $3.5 million suit against Mr Drapeau including the following statement:

> ... 2 The plaintiffs categorically deny with the greatest vigour the above mentioned accusations of the defendant towards them and assert that they are not inciters of violence, that they do not sanction the overthrow of established institutions by force, and that they have no relationship with any terrorist movement of any sort, including the Front de liberation du Québec (FLQ), having instead adopted democratic means and the electoral route to extol their ideas and their programmes.
>
> 5 The citizen's committees and the worker's unions which support the Front d'action politique, are not organizations which incite to violence, nor the overthrow of established institutions by force, and these same remarks apply to other supporters of this organization.
>
> 7 *d* This same resolution of the permanent council of the Front d'action politique simply adopts certain objectives of the manifesto of the Front de libération du Québec, but does not in any way endorse the means adopted by the Front de libération du Québec to put the manifesto into effect. On the contrary, this same resolution extolled democratic methods and the electoral route to put the various objectives of the Front de libération du Québec and the platform of the Front d'action politique into effect.

Claude Ryan's editorial appeal to the provincial government to cancel the election was rejected, and on October 25 after a heavy turnout Mayor Drapeau received 92 per cent of the votes cast and won every seat. In a victory speech that night, Mayor Drapeau declared that "the vote expressed approval of the measures taken during the tragic moments of the last weeks ... the tragic circumstances of the last three weeks could have modified the course of history – there was a provisional committee that was going to take power by way of revolution. But the population was not

Toronto Daily Star, October 21, 1970

ready to follow misguided preachers who are not responsible to the citizens. It was a comprehensive vote on a comprehensive issue." Mayor Drapeau thanked the electors for rejecting "not only the known attacks made by revolutionaries but also the attempts to set up a provisional government charged with carrying out the transfer of constitutional powers to the revolutionary régime." (It was not clear whether Drapeau was referring to FRAP or to Mr Ryan's discussions about a new government, later to become the famous provisional government plot with his reference to a provisional committee.)

René Lévesque saw the election as "the last stage in a complete freeze-up of democracy in the city." A day later in a major policy statement, "One can no longer wait," he asked Bourassa to call the National Assembly into session to begin a massive campaign of "collective re-education" and frontal attack on the major social, economic, and political problems facing the province. The Parti québécois, he declared, was willing to accept "partial responses," although it believed that only independence could provide ultimate solutions. The failure to launch a constructive attack on the causes of discontent, warned Lévesque, would be "further sowing the seeds of revolt and fury among people whose only wish is to be respected and live decently." As an opening move he called for the "public and private powers" to cease "the distortion and the calumny which they and those they control have heaped on the people and groups with whom they do not agree." Mayor Drapeau's charge that a parallel government was preparing to take power on the eve of the Montreal election, Lévesque described as "the most sinister farce."

As calm slowly returned to Montreal, opposition spokesmen and the press became increasingly insistent that the government more fully justify its belief in an "apprehended insurrection." But however shrill and insistent was the opposition, and above all the Canadian left, every indicator suggested that the public was firmly behind the use of the War Measures Act. On November 15 Omnifacts conducted a survey in Quebec for CTV which suggested that 84.8 per cent supported the action while only 9.6 per cent were opposed. On November 27 a poll conducted for *La Presse* revealed that 72.8 per cent supported and 15.6 per cent opposed the War Measures Act, a change which was variously described as marking a shift in opinion or the accident of the sample. On December 19 the Canadian Institute of Public Opinion published the answers to the following question:

We are interested in finding out how people felt that some of our political leaders conducted themselves in the recent FLQ crisis. Did your opinion of these men go up or down as a result of what they did, or said?

	Up	Down	The same	Can't say
Pierre Elliott Trudeau	60%	5%	30%	5%
Robert Bourassa	45	7	29	19
Réal Caouette	19	13	36	32
John Robarts	17	9	42	32
Robert Stanfield	11	23	49	17
Tommy Douglas	8	36	35	21

If the polls were accurate, they suggested that the renewed activity of the Parti québécois in November was largely ineffective. Addressing a regional PQ conference on November 8 René Lévesque had charged Trudeau and the federal government with fascist manipulation:

> For them the kidnappings have served merely as a pretext, nothing more than to stifle the people by manipulation. Hitler didn't come to power by using force ...
>
> However, men like Marchand, Trudeau, and Drapeau and the people around them have taken advantage of the October events to seize Quebec and turn the Quebec government into a puppet.
>
> This was a manipulation of the people of Quebec and Trudeau behaved like a fascist manipulator. Fascism means a taste for absolute power which suffers no answers, the coercion of outsiders into the ranks. Trudeau justified his War Measures by saying: tomorrow it could be a farmer, a child (he mentioned children twice), the manager of a savings bank. All that to manipulate the people. The more nervous he is, the more broadcasts Trudeau makes. There were calculated errors, when he mentioned people who don't agree (like me and Ryan, who were both for negotiation) and wondering whether we wern't in sympathy with the FLQ. That's all the same type of dirty fascist manipulation as Caouette uses. Both of them can be ranked together as fascist manipulators ...
>
> We don't have to make any excuses for what has happened. We tore our hearts out trying to uproot the FLQ and redirect it. But who poisoned democracy? Trudeau, the federal "gang" and federal finance which manipulated the April elections, which tried to crush the PQ even though we wanted to avoid any violence. These professional hypocrites tried to make out FLQ and PQ were one then. Today some of the political slobs are holding a hand out to the PQ when five months ago they did everything to destroy a decision which made good collective sense.
>
> Now they are reaping what they sowed. The PQ doesn't have to make any excuses. It just has to make itself legally accepted as a legitimate party while waiting for an end to be made to a system which encourages unhealthy FLQ extremism on the one hand and displaced persons like Trudeau on the other.

On November 15 Pierre Bourgault had appealed to three hundred party faithful to "speak out. We have enough strength to start a real fight against the fascist system ... Don't forget that the army is here, and it's here to muzzle us ... Speak up! Show them you exist. The worst that can happen is that you lose your job or go to jail – it's not so terrible – especially if it means that in five, ten, or fifteen years we can speak freely of the free Quebec we are all working for."

The voters in Labelle and Frontenac, however, left little doubt where they stood in two November 17 by-elections. In Labelle, where the total vote was down, the Liberals increased their margin substantially. The Liberals had lost Frontenac to the Créditistes by three thousand votes in

1968, and the Péquistes had shown considerable strength in the area on April 29. But on November 17, helped perhaps by the presence of a dozen MPs and three cabinet ministers, the Liberals defeated the Créditistes by six thousand votes.

On November 26 Mr Lévesque was the featured speaker at a rally of three thousand called by the Quebec Committee for the Protection of Civil Liberties . He warned that within two to five years "Quebec's economic, political, and social system will sink into a permanent confrontation between anarchy and repression if we don't manage to change it." But nothing could be expected from Bourassa, a machine made "to ensure the continuation of an exploited people, of a society fed by the present disorder and conditioned to resignation" or from Trudeau, a "grim old conservative out of the museum of political and socio-economic antiquities of federal Canada, firmly entrenched in his traditional contempt for the French nation of Quebec." The meeting itself called for the halt of "police repression," the end of unjustified arrests and searches, and "liberation of prisoners of war and eventually of political prisoners, who in the most arbitrary fashion are presumed guilty retroactively for essentially political acts and declarations, who have never been declared to be criminals under the Criminal Code."

The Last Act

OCTOBER 27–DECEMBER 28

AS Ottawa and Quebec grew increasingly impatient with the slow work of the police and the combined anti-terrorist forces were slowly adding to the list of those questioned or detained, the audacity of the FLQ cells continued. Another communiqué was issued on October 27, which not only bore the fingerprint of Paul Rose but contained his passport:

October 27, 1970
Joint communiqué of the Chenier, Liberation, and Dieppe cells.

The Front de libération du Québec wishes to clarify several items of information regarding the ideas and intentions attributed to it by the ruling authorities.

As defined in the manifesto, the Front is not seeking political power. The FLQ is formed of groups of workers who have decided to take a step towards the revolution, the only real way for the workers to achieve and exercise power. This revolution will not be carried out by some one hundred people, as the ruling authorities would like everyone to believe, but by *all the population.* Real people's power is exercised by the people and for the people. The FLQ leaves the coups d'état to the three ruling governments, since these same seem to be past masters in this field. Our ancestors are not the Fathers of Confederation, they are the patriots of 1837–38. Our fathers, our big brothers, our uncles are not the Bordens, the St Laurents, the Duplessis; they are the boys who were massacred at Dieppe for having been forced to serve as guinea pigs, as "cheap labour," they are the boys who were bludgeoned at Murdochville and elsewhere for having wanted to defend their rights to exist. Our brothers today are not the Trudeaus, the Bourassas, the Drapeaus, they are the guys from Lapalme, the guys who will be killed shortly by Bill 38, all the exploited people of Quebec.

The FLQ is formed of groups of workers who have formed themselves the aim of fighting to the end the daily acts of state terrorism. The fault of the FLQ, in the eyes of the ruling authorities, is not so much the use of violence but the use of violence against the establishment. It is this in particular that is unpardonable. It is this in particular that creates fear.

The establishment has everything to gain in communicating this fear to the general population. Firstly, to justify an armed intervention in Quebec, which, they think, will assure them (the establishment) a certain protection. Then to show the Quebec people that they must forget forever any idea of total liberation.

But the Front de libération du Québec knows that the population is not a sucker to such a game, even if the different governments mobilize everything in order to claim the contrary. For example, this is what they have attempted in the case of the results of the Montreal elections.

On this topic we wish to briefly reveal a few concluding facts: the high percentage of Anglophone vote that was expressed, the high level of abstentions in working class ridings, and the percentage of the vote granted to the worker candidates in these same ridings. These facts having been made clear, one realizes that the Civic party and its "leader" were elected with the support of hardly 10 per cent of the population. This is what we dare call democracy.

Québécois, the time of deceptions is over.

Québécois, the English and French upper bourgeoisies have spoken; it is now time for us to act.

Liberation, Chenier, and Dieppe cells.

We shall overcome.

Front de libération du Québec.

P.S. 1 No impediment on behalf of the ruling police authorities should hinder the free publication of this communiqué.

2 As long as the police forces apply a partial or total censure to the publication of the present communiqué, no communication from the Liberation cell will reach them.

The Suspects

By this time the police had clearly identified the wanted men – Paul Rose and his brother Jacques, Marc Carbonneau, Jacques Lanctôt, Francis Simard, and Bernard Lortie. To assist discovery the governments of Canada and Quebec on November 2 offered a total joint reward of $150,000 for information leading to the arrest of the kidnappers. Three days later the FLQ issued pictures of Cross playing solitaire on a case labelled explosives. Meanwhile, following the murder of Laporte, the Rose brothers and Simard had moved in with a girl friend of Jacques', Colette Therrien, and her two friends Francine and François Belisle, where they were joined by Bernard Lortie. The men constructed a false wall in a large closet, and it was there they fled on the night of November 6 when police knocked on the door. Lortie had not time to enter and was arrested, as were the others found in the apartment. The next morning Lortie testified at the Laporte inquest, admitting that he had participated in the kidnapping but stating that he had left the Armstrong Street house the day before the murder. As Lortie testified, the police ransacked the apartment as the three suspects sat motionless in their hiding place. When the police left for dinner Saturday night, the men escaped. It was not the first time the FLQ humiliated the Montreal police, who had once lost Rose a few days before the murder.

Testimony at the inquest by Paul Rose's girl friend, Lise Balcer, the

Therriens, and others filled out the picture of the Chenier cell from early discussions about a kidnapping to the escape from the apartment. Meanwhile, the three members of the cell continued to mock the police by issuing another communiqué, this time over the name of the Viger (another 1837 patriote) cell describing their escape and demanding that Lortie be added to the list of "political prisoners" whose release they still demanded:

Saturday, November 14
Front de libération du Québec
Information Viger Cell Communiqué no 2

The Viger information cell in collaboration with the Chenier financial cell sends you this communiqué to make clear the events surrounding the arrest of Bernard Lortie. It is of general interest to provide some particulars on the subject of various information which has circulated in the established newspapers.

1 Contrary to what the present authorities want to be believed, Bernard Lortie did not squeal and did not betray. He acted as he should have (this will be confirmed by what follows). For this reason his name must be added to the twenty-three political prisoners whose release is called for by the FLQ.

2 Here are the facts (proving the authenticity of this document): notice to Fuhrer St Pierre.

A When the police turned up on Friday, November 6, there were inside the apartment in addition to two young girls, our four sought-after comrades.

B The fascist police knocked, then smashed down the door (as is their habit). The two girls and Bernard Lortie (who was in an ordinary wardrobe) were caught. The three others had time to conceal themselves in a hiding place which they had previously constructed (a hiding place which was in a wardrobe).

C The three patriots stayed motionless for twenty-four hours.

D On Saturday evening at 6:30 PM the two policemen left to have supper leaving their weapons in the apartment. It was at this moment that our three comrades fled by the rear door of the apartment which was locked from the inside. They did not forget to take with them the weapons left through a negligent oversight. The Front thanks them for it.

E Before leaving the place Francis Simard, Jacques Rose, and his brother Paul took care not to close the entrance to their hiding place again and left their fingerprints everywhere. In spite of that the police have not disclosed the facts and preferred to make Bernard Lortie look like a traitor to shatter the sympathy of the public for the FLQ.

F The Chenier cell continues to fight.

We shall overcome, FLQ.

A week later a final communiqué was sent to *Le Journal de Montréal* and *Québec-Presse* enclosing a letter from Mr Cross but clearly dictated by his hosts:

Front de libération du Québec, November 21, 1970.
Viger Information Cell, Communiqué no 3.

The Liberation cell has asked us to forward the two enclosed letters written by the political prisoner J. Cross.

One letter is public. This letter is addressed neither to the Anglo-Saxon racists, nor to the various small dictators, nor to the Trudeau-Choquette styled fascist apprentices, but specifically to those who still have some dignity and fight in them. This letter is the testimony of a man who, during the past few weeks, has lost some of his illusions.

The other letter is personal and is addressed to Mrs Cross.

The Viger cell also wants to outline the position of the FLQ towards certain recent events and statements:

1 The fascist political police seem to have "voted" themselves new powers. After the failure of thousands of door-to-door searches, hundreds of arrests, of censorship, these SS fell back upon a dismally famous practice – torture. This is not new, but aside from being barbaric, primitive, and inhuman, this tactic is useless because we anticipated it and acted accordingly. The FLQ knows its torturers.

2 Mr U Thant has called upon the Front de libération du Québec to free J. Cross. If Mr Thant really wants to save the life of this man and if he wants to comply with the humanitarian principles that he says he is defending, he must then adopt a position on the liberation struggle of the people of Quebec, the peoples of Latin America, Asia, Africa, and of the black people in Amerikka [*sic*]; he must restore dignity to the UN by condemning the interventionist politics practised by the imperialist and racist powers; he must condemn torture in Quebec and throughout the world; he must propose himself as intermediary between the FLQ and the Canadian government to speed the liberation of the twenty-four Québécois political prisoners and of the political prisoner J. Cross. In making this gesture, he will proceed from "fine" words to action.

3 We also wish to make it very clear to all those gentlemen of the "small" newspapers who, having only dollar signs in their heads, publish all sorts of crazy rumours and engage in a small war of big headlines, that they are not managing to discredit the FLQ amongst the workers. The latter fully realize that these men are not interested in publishing certain shocking truths (slums, unemployment, corruption, etc.) which are found in profusion in "la Belle Province." We have no secret negotiations with any government whatsoever; we leave the secret dealings to employers and the governments.

We shall overcome, FLQ.

November 15
To whom it may concern:

I want to assure those who are interested (if there are still some) that I am in good health and being well treated. I have heard about the treatment of FLQ political prisonners [*sic*] in jail and I am quite sure that I am better treated than them. I have all the information possible – radio, TV, newspapers. I have "hot" dinners every day. I also have my pills.

I can wash and have clean clothes and I have not been questioned. But time drags very heavily after six weeks of imprisonment.

They consider me as a political prisonner [*sic*] and they will keep me in captivity as long as the authorities do not accept their demands.

I have heard my wife on the radio a few weeks ago. I know it must be very hard and painful for her. But it must be the same for the FLQ political prisonners [*sic*].

To whom and on what depend my liberty and my life I don't know. But I am still hoping.

J. R. Cross

P.S. I join to this public letter a private letter to my wife.

By this time, as the twenty-one-day limit expired, those arrested had been brought into court. On November 5 the first twenty-four appeared before a judge. The famous Montreal Five – Lemieux, Vallières, Gagnon, Chartrand, and Larue-Langlois – were charged with seditious conspiracy and membership in the FLQ. Predictably the courtroom became a political forum, the five challenging the jurisdiction of the court and hurling obscenities at the judge, Bourassa, and Trudeau. Vallières left the courtroom with upraised fist: "We shall overcome. Long live the FLQ." All were remanded until January 1971. By the end of the year 468 had been arrested, of whom 408 had been released without charges being laid. Some had been released on bail, but forty-one remained in prison, among them all the close friends and alleged accomplices of the Laporte murderers. Of the Montreal Five only Larue-Langlois had been granted bail, despite the crown prosecutor's objections. Two men had been sentenced: François Mercier, a Granby school teacher, for membership in the FLQ; and André Lavoie, a twenty-two-year-old Ottawa student, for conspiracy to commit a holdup for the Front.

Back to the Hill

Meanwhile, the government had lived up to its promise to replace the War Measures Act when John Turner introduced the Public Order Temporary Measures Act on November 2. While most of its clauses were taken from the earlier regulations, the new bill was limited to the FLQ, reduced the "presumptions of affiliation with the illegal association" as Mr Turner expressed it, added some legal safeguards for those arrested, and was to expire on April 30, 1971. Although the Conservatives supported the measure, Mr. Stanfield pointed to three defects during the November 4 debate on second reading: retroactivity, the absence of any provision for a judicial or independent review, and the ninety-day detention before those arrested had to be brought to trial. Mr Douglas agreed that the bill was an improvement on the old regulations, but described it as "arbitrary and repressive." Like Mr Stanfield the NDP leader found the retroactive clause and the reverse onus of proof objectionable. The press agreed with the opposition critics, and W.A. Wilson (*Montreal Star*,

Changing of the guard

Ottawa Citizen, December 2, 1970

November 3) warned that convictions under the retroactive clause would create martyrs and win adherents to the FLQ or some successor organization. After a two-day debate the House approved the bill in principle 152 to 1, with Conservative David MacDonald the sole opponent. The NDP decision to support the bill was reached after several agonizing caucus meetings, where the MP s undoubtedly weighed their dislike of the bill against another backlash of public disapproval of their stand. But Stanley Knowles declared that the NDP would force a lengthy debate unless the government agreed to several amendments that would eliminate the retroactive clause and increase the legal protection of those arrested.

The debate was lengthy, as the opposition used the occasion to con-

Armchair quarterback

Gazette, Montreal, November 12, 1970

tinue to demand more information on the apprehended insurrection. Not only did they secure none but Mr Turner refused to accept NDP and Conservative amendments. Although the opposition's demand that an administrator review, and report to Parliament on, the operation of the new and old measures was endorsed by the Liberal party's national policy conference on November 23, the government was inflexible. The Prime Minister argued that such an appointment would not only show a lack of confidence in the integrity of the Quebec government, but would encourage the separatist charge that "Ottawa is running the show and calling the shots in Quebec."

During the debate the NDP moved away from its earlier position. Some observers interpreted the move as a reflection of growing public scepticism about the alleged insurrection in Quebec, particularly when Bernard Lortie's testimony revealed that the Laporte kidnapping was hardly the work of a group with the capacity to overthrow the government of Quebec. Opposition critics were not the only skeptics. On December 10 the Canadian Civil Liberties Association demanded a royal commission to investigate the grounds on which the government acted, and resolved to establish such a commission itself if the demand was refused. The association also demanded repeal of the Public Order Act, branding it as unnecessary, misguided, and repressive.

In a surprise move the hard-line law and order members of the Ralliement créditiste also began to criticize the bill in the last days of debate. Créditiste spokesmen argued that its application to Quebec alone was an insult, that it was an attempt to "gag" opposition in the province, and that it did nothing to resolve the fundamental social and economic crisis in the province. Finally, on December 1 the bill passed 174 to 31, with two Conservatives joining the NDP and the Ralliement in opposition.

Several weeks earlier some of the estimated 7,500 troops began to leave the province. And on December 23 Prime Minister Trudeau said that he and Mr Bourassa had agreed that with the exception of some personal bodyguards all troops would be removed by January 4, 1971.

Cross Recovered

James Cross had been home for a month by then, and his kidnappers were safely in Cuba. After several days of investigation, the police and army surrounded an apartment at 10945 rue des Récollets early on December 3. The discovery appears to have been made by the RCMP who, through a combination of tips and shadowing, ultimately found Jacques Cossette-Trudel and his wife Louise (née Lanctôt). For about a week the police had watched the building, uncertain as to whether Mr Cross was inside. On the afternoon of December 2 the police arrested the Cossette-Trudels after they left the apartment, hoping to seize other inhabitants as they emerged. But later another man entered, assumed to be the mysterious Pierre (Seguin), mentioned in the testimony of witnesses at the Laporte murder, who later turned out to be Yves Langlois, a former stenographer for the Superior Court and the Quebec Police Commission. By midnight the police decided to close in and the electricity was turned off. Soon afterwards the kidnappers hurled a pipe through the window, with a note enclosed:

If you try anything at all (gas, gunfire, etc.) M.J. Cross will be the first to die. We have several sticks of "detonated" dynamite (powerfrac). So if you want to negotiate send us a reporter from *Québec-Presse* or the *Devoir* plus Mr B. Mergler.

We shall overcome, FLQ.

And as a last gesture of defiance, the Libération cell painted the letters FLQ on the front window.

By 8:30 in the morning the area was cordoned off and a neighbouring school closed, inhabitants moved off the street, and army canteens and a medical team set up, and trucks from the Montreal fire department and hundreds of heavily armed police and troops surrounded the FLQ fortress. The Cuban Embassy was alerted and the Canadian Pavilion at Man and His World became an extension of the embassy. Awakened early in the morning, Bernard Mergler agreed to negotiate. At 11 AM he entered the apartment and found Marc Carbonneau, Jacques Lanctôt, and Yves Langlois. Mr Mergler was easily able to establish Mr Cross' identity. He agreed to safe passage to Cuba for Jacques Lanctôt's wife and child and the captured Cossette-Trudels and finally persuaded the kidnappers not to insist on extensive press coverage for the trip to the island. At 12:55, surrounded on all sides by motorcycles and police cars, the battered 1962 Chrysler began its journey, the kidnappers carrying six sticks of dynamite and two M1 semi-automatic rifles and a pistol. By eight o'clock that evening the kidnappers were bound for Cuba. At 1:07 AM on Friday, December 4, they were admitted to Cuba, and James Cross was finally free. Behind they left tapes of conversations, presumably held as they waited for their inevitable discovery, where they examined their accomplishments. The document, published in *Choc* (December), is fascinating:

B

... We really thought the government was ready ... that it was going to agree. When we did the kidnapping we said: "Maybe in four or five days, a week at the outside, the government will agree to negotiate." What can you make of that, the all-out refusal, the final no of Trudeau ... Bourassa ... and then what has our action achieved so far?

A

What I mean ... it's not one of the main things ... but I have the feeling with these kidnappings in Quebec, there's something, there's one factor which was important during the crisis. And this was that they didn't want our tactics to succeed ... they didn't want Central America's tactics [to] come up north ... in other words they know the problems the Black Panthers, the Weathermen, all those people have in the United States ... the problems the Front has in Quebec ... and I get the feeling they didn't want an overspill from South America and get the same problems: yeah, that was the main thing. It's not the first time the government in Washington, let's say, gave a personal warning to Trudeau, not to say yes, 'cause that would create a precedent ... and then he in turn would be overwhelmed by Black Panthers.

I get the feeling that there was advice from Washington. There's also the matter ... maybe this is a bit more personal ... but Trudeau's personality counted for a great deal. It may all be part of a strategical plan ... but Trudeau, we know all about his theories on federation and he is in no way prepared to accept giving anything away to any bit of territory or to any kind of nationalism ... That's sure for a start.

B

If it had been Pearson or Stanfield ... or another government chief ... anybody else but Trudeau ... you could say he would probably have accepted negotiations and liberation of the prisoners.

A

Yeah sure ... don't forget Trudeau had to think of the Anglophones' opinions ... then straightaway I think ... the *Star*, the day after the kidnapping, decided no one should give in to blackmail; Quebec's Anglophones wanted the problem settled once and for all.

B

Another thing I think was to do with all the people who felt threatened ... What I mean is Trudeau tried to make people believe in his little dictator speeches, his brief television appearances ... to try and destroy the sympathy that the Québécois ... that many, many Québécois felt for the FLQ patriots ... I feel Trudeau was getting a big push from the "big bosses," the "big shots" from the west, people who have nothing whatsoever to do with Quebec.

A

Another thing ... as far as I am concerned this is the main thing anyway ... and that's that we were double-crossed by the federal government ... I mean the federal government stirred up the city much more than we thought they could ... because they saw there was a chance of tying up Quebec's progressive forces.

B

Then there were the municipal elections in Montreal ... And remember that political life in Montreal is very, very important within Quebec, because it's a bit ... revolutionary activity has been more obvious in Montreal than elsewhere. I get the feeling they wanted to wipe FRAP out by making the struggle seem radical ... by bringing about collective hysteria which, on a short-term basis, made people drift towards the strongest side.

We could mention one victory so far ... 'cause one of our chief demands was met: the broadcasting of the manifesto ... which attracted a lot of sympathy. For the first time, patriots of the Front managed to express themselves by entering every home, through Radio-Canada, which read our manifesto ... They were in touch for the first time, although it was a rough and ready way to do it. That was when they began to understand ... What I mean is before you only got into Quebec homes through the big sensation-monger papers or through papers like *La Presse* ... controlled by Power Corporation ... who explained to us the way they wanted. So when bombs exploded in Westmount they put their own meaning on it, then they tried to terrorize the Québécois as much as the Anglophones. But making them read our manifesto, well, let's say that stirred it up ... it made our intentions clear ... The Minister of Regional Expansion for the federal government, Marchand, told the press, after the manifesto was read ... he said all the federal cabinet was surprised, even astonished to see the popular support the manifesto received. You can explain that because the federal government was so out of touch with Quebec's problems and the Québécois that it didn't believe the demands made by the people for two years were urgent. Then, when they saw the manifesto brought about a shock effect, brought people over to our side, I think that's when Trudeau's government decided to settle the whole matter by using their lackey in Quebec: Bourassa.

D

All in all, the government is making a big mistake if they think they can kill us by military means. The FLQ is not an army to be fought like that. The whole population belongs to the FLQ. Every guy who commits one small action to benefit Quebec's society is a member of the FLQ, and in fact is doing the same as us.

A

Just now ... I said the FLQ was primarily a revolutionary organization, that it was more or less sporadic. I don't mean the Front forgot everything that went before. Not at all ... we all owe something to what has gone before. We even use the Front de libération ... but as far as I am concerned the Front's organization seems different to the public this year than it was previously:

I mean in the Cross-Laporte business, I think you see a very good example of co-operation between two FLQ cells: the Chenier cell and the Liberation cell ... and latterly the Viger cell, communications ... which is very active, which includes a fair number of supporters.

These cells communicate with each other very cautiously, on a very personal level. But I believe that this business of communication between the different cells of the Front is altogether new. The cells were never able to communicate before. It's pretty sure that within Quebec, because of the nature of the FLQ, you couldn't say all the FLQ cells are in touch with each other, 'cause a cell of the FLQ grows from among citizens, among workers who want to advance their cause more quickly and it's pretty difficult to get in touch with those guys because of the dangers of cell-formation. But I think that so far, this year anyway, the Front is much better organized, better structured, and it's working in a more responsible and security-conscious way. Another thing ... this year ... I don't think the Front de libération has had a lengthy silence like there was before, last year.

"S'il vous plait, Marc, explain to me again about our great moral victory."

Chronicle-Herald, Halifax, December 8, 1970

If you want to talk about the FLQ that's a bit touchy because we don't want to count our chickens before they're hatched. But for what it's worth, let's say ... it's a group of workers from all walks of life ... which has operated ... not necessarily within organizations like citizens' committees or workmen's committees, in some factories and industries ... that happened a lot ... but it's more a confrontation of people in meetings, under observation ... what I mean is you could see that such and such a person was heading in such and such a political direction ... and you got further with that person and you ended up forming a cell which started recruiting members.

That's more or less what has happened so far. Obviously there was no systematic recruitment into the FLQ. Well, that hasn't happened so far. The numbers involved ... I think it might be wiser not to mention that just now. Maybe all we can say is that the FLQ has enough sympathizers and active members to present a real threat to the powers that be and to the financiers hiding in there.

C

What do you think of the PQ's action just now?

B

The PQ sure is a good reserve for future Félquistes; no doubt whatsoever. Because if you watch the way things are going, it's quite clear that the Péquiste hopes are going to be dashed pretty quickly: you only have to look at how the seven Péquiste members of Parliament are treated in the House. Personally I don't agree at all with the PQ ideology ... except for the wish to be independent it expresses. But you must make a distinction between Péquiste organizations and Péquiste sympathizers. I prefer the sympathizers to the Péquiste organizers. My feeling is that people will soon see that a democratic way that means too many concessions in the party's programme, too many concessions in the struggles in which it engages ... I think people – well, you can see the signs already – there's no doubt, they'll get tired of that way.

A

At any rate, Pierre Bourgault said that if in six months "democracy" hadn't proved itself conclusively ... in six months plenty of Parti québécois supporters will be candidates for the Front de libération du Québec ... will be prepared to stand up for the same acts of principle for direct action as the Front does right now.

The Parti québécois is after all ... let's say its programme is not too clear. You could say first of all it wants independence for Quebec ... but as for the economy, it doesn't suggest any useful solution ... to bring about the real liberation of the people of Quebec. That means that politically speaking we would no longer be tied to Ottawa, but we would still be dependent on Wall Street ... so that means the same financiers ... Rockefeller said it anyway ... what it means is that, as far as Rockefeller is concerned, whether we are independent or not, everything remains the same for him ... He'll go on investing in Quebec and run our mines, our natural resources ... things like that. The lords will still be able to fish in their private lakes ... So the PQ stands for political independence but ... in the Québécois minds; it doesn't yet mean economic independence ... Then the front wants economic and social independence as well as political independence. What this boils down to is that we must stop being milked by these financiers ... In other words we must stop being the reserve strength of the Americans. In any case our political independence must go hand in hand with economic independence. We must stop being a source of reserve strength and take over our own resources, our industries and our mines at the same time as we take over our politics.

A

In fact you could say the PQ ... I think the PQ wouldn't change much ... just the exploitation we've suffered from in Quebec since the beginning ... since we've been here after all! The exploitation we suffer from now would only get a moral face lift. It would be hidden behind more Quebec-orientated power, a little more human maybe ...

The difference between the FLQ and the PQ and other leftist movements as far as I am concerned is the way it acts so it is a far more violent and radical outfit than we have seen in Quebec for years.

B

Well our methods of action are pretty well recognized so far. You could say there are bomb attacks which aren't made to really kill the people who live in Westmount or any other capitalist hangouts, but more to frighten them.

Sure bomb attacks are dangerous ... because it's a double-edged weapon. It can all come back on us because the newspapers, the almighty press ... sure, as soon as there is a bomb attack, the almighty press gets hold of it all to frighten Québécois ... when the real object of the attack is to frighten a few to make them go home to their mother country, Ottawa ... or to make them think about exploitation.

A

I believe those tactics showed results in May and June ... I feel just after the bomb attacks in Westmount, where seven bombs exploded ... more than that were laid. In the days after that ... or even next day, plenty of Westmount people decided to pack up and if you went through the streets of Westmount a week later, you could see that one house out of three was for sale and the "big bosses" and the top guys had gone into hiding a bit further to the west of the island ... I hope they were getting out, going back to where they came from: to Ontario, or Great Britain, or the United States.

B

You should make it clear too that those attacks weren't aggressions in themselves but more an answer to aggression. Don't forget that it wasn't the Front that started the fighting. We have been subjected to humiliation, hate, and racism by the Anglophones for two hundred years. One of the main short-term objectives of the FLQ is to strip power of all its trappings and bring it out in the open. Apart from bomb attacks you need to open up ... carry out actions that are more and more spectacular, like the Palestinians. I think you could go so far as to say, even if you were careful ... because we have received fairly well inside information ... but I believe you could say the Front has a lot in common with the National Liberation Front in Algeria ... and Quebec's problems are in some ways a lot like the ones Algeria had before independence.

(...) It's not hard to see that the action of the Front de libération du Québec at certain times and in certain ways found its inspiration in the National Liberation Front ... the FNL ... in Algeria. Maybe that explains why we chose the place we did as a place of exile for the political prisoners we want to free ... we chose Cuba or Algeria ... hoping no doubt it would turn out to be Algeria ... 'cause it's a country where French is spoken and where ... it was a land which in many ways had the same problems as Quebec ... and our imprisoned political comrades might have sometimes found the solutions or the explanations ... or some guidance or examples of how to solve conflicts.

F

In ending we say: "Long live free Quebec!" "Long live our imprisoned political comrades!" ... "Long live the revolution in Quebec!" and "Long live the Front de libération du Québec!"

For more than three weeks the executioners of Pierre Laporte continued to evade the police. From their closet hideaway on Queen Mary Road the three men moved to another address in Montreal, where they remained for three days before being driven, with food for ten days, to St Bonaventure, sixty-five miles east of Montreal. There they remained for at least ten days, while friends sought another refuge. Finally they located an empty farmhouse near St Luc on rue l'Acadie, twenty miles southwest of Montreal. The house had been rented in September by Michel Viger, a thirty-one-year-old Longueuil insurance salesman who as president of the south shore committee of the defunct Rassemblement pour l'indépendance nationale had met Paul Rose several years before.

Michel Viger had been picked up in the wave of arrests following the proclamation of the War Measures Act but soon released. The house had been noticed by St Luc police, however, and was being watched, particularly after police activity on the south shore increased around the middle of December. Mr Viger was detained again on December 23, and that evening police raided the house but found no signs of life. On Christmas Day, after Mr Viger had been released and had been seen leaving the farm, the police again searched the house. A sleeping bag and a shovel with fresh dirt on it was sufficient evidence to mount a stakeout, with police posing as snowmobilers. Another search at 4:40 on December 27 yielded nothing, but four hours later the police arrived to find Mr Viger at home. After questioning and undoubtedly realizing the game was up, he led police to concrete bricks hiding a twenty-foot tunnel dug under the basement floor. He rapped on the bricks and called "Paul." A voice answered "Oui." According to police Mr Viger said: "If you want to die, I will die with you. But that's wrong. Our cause is a good one, Paul. You are still needed."

Threatened with a shoot-out, the police agreed to negotiate, and after several men were vetoed both sides accepted as negotiator Dr Jacques Ferron, a doctor, novelist, and RIN candidate in 1966. The kidnappers continued to demand that the prisoners be released to prevent more deaths, but the most that Jacques Ducros agreed to for the government was that bail for those in jail would no longer be automatically opposed, but would be determined by the courts. By dawn on December 28 it was over.

Questions and Consequences

THE CRISIS was over, but the debate was not – and perhaps never would be. The major issues around which political and public controversy centred were the unwillingness of the governments to negotiate the freedom of the twenty-three criminals; the alleged subordination of Quebec to Ottawa; the reasons for the use of the army and the War Measures Act; and the intermediate and long-term effects of the crisis on both the governments and society of Quebec and Canada and their future relations.

Some Canadians believed and continued to believe that the governments should have freed the twenty-three prisoners for the release of James Cross and Pierre Laporte. Led by Claude Ryan and René Lévesque and joined by such English Canadians as George Bain (*Canadian Forum*, January 1971), they repeatedly insisted that it had been the inflexible government in Ottawa that had prevented such negotiations and had ultimately resulted in Laporte's death. There was no direct contemporary evidence to support such a hypothesis, nor could much in the way of inference be drawn from the actions of either government. Spokesmen for both governments were direct and unanimous that consideration had never been given to the release of the twenty-three. (Had it been a question only of the manifesto and the ransom, Gérard Pelletier wrote later, "negotiation would have been fairly easy" (*La crise d'octobre*). The fullest statement of the Quebec position was given by Jérôme Choquette in the National Assembly on November 12:

> ... our guiding principle was to safeguard the essence of our democratic society and our judicial system, while at the same time trying to be as flexible as possible.
>
> The reasons for taking this attitude were as follows:
>
> Firstly, these were not political prisoners, inasmuch as they had all been condemned or were under accusation by virtue of our civil law.
>
> Secondly, had we given in to the basic demands we would have been condoning the system of kidnapping or abduction and would have wrecked a judicial system which – in spite of all that is said about it – is one of the most impartial in the world.
>
> Thirdly, methods of contestation prevailing in a democratic society auto-

matically exclude violence as a form of pressure, be it in accordance with the decisions of our elected representatives, or with decisions made by the judiciary.

Fourthly, violence breeds violence and, consequently, anarchy. At this stage it is no longer law and the decisions of the lawcourts but force and violence which determine what is just and what is unjust.

Fifthly, to have surrendered to such disgusting blackmail, without safeguarding the principle of order which is the basis of the exercise of liberty, would have opened the way to a growth of such methods.

Sixthly, and finally, how in all decency could we have dealt with any subsequent cases against terrorists or others by virtue of our laws? We know that the phenomenon of terrorism is not an isolated one. We have experienced it since 1963 and what has happened is only the culmination of these vague terrorist actions in the past. Who would have wished to use such methods to solve any problems or to deal with situations involving protest?

However, we offered to be flexible in some respects for the following reasons:

Firstly, and primarily, to save Mr Cross' life.

Secondly, to pacify the atmosphere created by the terrorist action, whatever its reasons.

Thirdly, to demonstrate humanity which was compatible with the respect due to the democratic will.

And yet many factors were unknown at that time.

Who were these revolutionaries? What were their intentions? How far were they prepared to go? Had they called a complete halt to their plans? By displaying a measure of understanding in the exercise of our responsibility we hoped to come half-way to these people who were unknown to us. In case we were dealing with idealists who had been led astray we offered them a line of survival and, it might be hoped, the lessening or elimination of terrorism in the future.

But if this was a carefully planned-out escalation, involving abduction and further developments in the area of social disturbance or murder, then I did not think that they would proceed immediately to murder James Cross. In this respect, several previous delays had been granted.

I was also counting on the support of the leaders of public opinion, but this was not forthcoming. To me it seems elementary that to have accepted the conditions imposed would have meant a landslide into anarchy. I also expected that there would be no politicking or playing around with such a serious matter as the respect for democratic institutions and the life of a man. I overestimated the powers of comprehension of our leaders of opinion.

Almost immediately one totally unexpected event took place – the abduction of Pierre Laporte. In the days which followed several things took place, including the meeting at the Paul Sauvé Arena. Like many other groups, this meeting expressed its support of the FLQ. Amongst other things opinions were expressed by FRAP and the central council of the CSN, Montreal. Tracts were distributed in various universities and CEGEPS. One order was given: go into the streets. But I was deeply impressed by Communiqué no 5 from the Chenier cell on October 12 at 3 PM which expressed the following ideas: two conditions to be fulfilled for the liberation of Mr Cross and six to free Mr Laporte; otherwise it meant execution for both, dependent on the number of requirements with which we would be prepared to comply.

Given the enormity of these requirements, the various conditions stipulated for the liberation of James Cross and Pierre Laporte and all the other circumstances to which I have referred – acceptance of blackmail, encouragement of subsequent terrorism, evidence of weakness on the government's part and, lastly, abdication from democratic and judiciary institutions in the face of crime, we could make no offer other than the one which I had previously proposed, to which I added a promise to recommend the immediate freeing of six prisoners who would be eligible at that time for conditional parole ...

Prime Minister Bourassa became incensed at the repeated charges that the cabinet was divided. At a hard-hitting press conference on October 29 he declared: "If there were any crises, there would have been resignations. Have there been any resignations?" "Show me," he asked reporters, "one iota of statements made by any minister, which would permit the writing of such articles." Interviewed by *Gazette* reporters on December 3 he replied to Mr Lévesque's statement that he had told him that the cabinet was divided: "I saw René Lévesque on television and he lied at least three times. I never said to him that the cabinet was divided; this is completely false. He said that ministers were locked in their basement and refused to come out. This is completely false. He said that he never asked for protection from the police. This is completely false. He asked for protection from the police." In the same interview Mr Bourassa gave his version of his government's position and in effect admitted that the cabinet was not united at the outset:

My reaction when Cross was kidnapped was that we could not yield to blackmail. My first reaction when Pierre Laporte was kidnapped was also that I could not see how we could yield to blackmail.

But I said we have to do something to save his life; perhaps we could try to negotiate. We certainly could not accept all their demands. Perhaps we could find a way out whereby the life of Pierre Laporte could be saved and without the security of the state being endangered. So that's why we accepted to negotiate. When I received the letter from Pierre – and you know it was a very personal letter – I said, "Well, this has to be a unanimous cabinet decision." I could not make decisions in that situation where we would have been divided let's say 9 to 6 or 13 to 12.

With the life of a colleague involved, I decided to take the time for discussion. We discussed it Sunday, Monday – very long discussions. Of course, at the beginning, there were different view points, but it was unanimous in the end ...

We accepted the principle of negotiation. We agreed to discuss with them to see exactly what they wanted and what kind of a compromise we could reach with them. First, we wanted to decide the prior question, the question of safe conduct. So you see, this had to be clear. And when we cleared that we were ready to discuss the demands, but not necessarily to accept them ...

But Lemieux was meeting Demers. Lemieux said something different to

Demers; something different still on television after that and it was humiliating for the government to see Lemieux on television saying: "I saw the government, and the government replied to me ..." Enough was enough, but we tried. We tried and we said: "it's impossible."

(In a November 3 interview Choquette, a leading hawk, admitted too that the cabinet was not united: "At the start not everybody was at the same point. There was a different way of seeing things ... we met Sunday for the first time and we had another meeting Monday; another Tuesday and so on ... it took three days ... I think it was Wednesday that there was agreement among everybody.")

In an interview in *Le magazine Maclean* (January 1971), Bourassa explained the differing tone of the government statements:

> We never accepted the principle of the freeing of the twenty-three prisoners ... How is it possible to surrender coldly to blackmail? But after Pierre's letter, I was involved ... The tone of my speech was different, its presentation was different. It did not mean that we were backing down on our principles, but I was not putting aside a change in the government's attitude. I was not putting aside negotiations. In effect, we made a significant change in our attitude: we were prepared to recommend the conditional parole of those prisoners who were so entitled.

Underlining that the decision was Quebec's, he observed in the Assembly

"I am not required to tell you anything but my name, rank, date of birth and social insurance number."

Chronicle-Herald, Halifax, November 2, 1970

on November 12 that under the procedure "nolle prosequi" Quebec alone could have released eleven of the twenty-three, but his government refused to do so.

Inside the House and out critics of the Trudeau and Bourassa administrations argued that the "apprehended insurrection" was a figment of the imagination. They saw nothing in the events of October 5–15 to suggest that civil government was in danger, or that Montreal faced civil disorders sufficiently grave to warrant the designation "apprehended insurrection." In the Commons the Prime Minister continued to state that the government acted on facts known to the public. In an interview with Louis Martin on "Format 60" on November 3, he elaborated slightly:

Q: For instance, in so far as the first act, the War Measures Act, is concerned, you wished to justify it by mentioning the abductions, the dynamite thefts, the appeals made by the city of Montreal and the provincial government; do you believe that it was established to your complete satisfaction – you have been asked the same question several times – that there was really a state of apprehended insurrection?
A: We know what insurrection is, don't we? But what is apprehended insurrection? I suppose it is an insurrection which responsible people apprehend.
Q: Does that therefore give them a great deal of latitude?
A: Of course, but this is how the law is devised, because one doesn't wait for the insurrection to have started and for five hundred people to have been shot in the streets, to say: Ah! There you are! It's insurrection. The same law covers war – whether it has been declared or is apprehended. During a period of war the War Measures Act doesn't wait until the enemy has arrived in the capital and has started cutting people's throats. In the minds of those in power it is when war is imminent that extreme measures must be taken and they act accordingly. So that, in this particular case, the apprehension of insurrection was unanimous. Not only on the part of the Quebec government, Montreal city leaders, and the federal government but also, if I am not wrong, on the part of all the Quebec representatives in Ottawa who voted in favour of this act. This implies that those who know Quebec said to themselves, it's serious: those guys who started with a hundred or so bomb attacks and who have killed half a dozen people, etc., have started making appeals for people to go into the street now. Then there was the business in the universities and the CEGEPS ... I believe that if the government had waited for all that to blow over, or if trouble had started, if maybe in defence of lives or goods pistol shots had been fired on one side or another and that there had been perhaps two deaths like in Kent State, then people would have said, after all, the government should have seen that coming, they should have done something earlier. They should have realized there was going to be trouble. So, at the back of everyone's mind who grasped the situation there was fear of trouble.

Justice Minister Choquette gave a fuller statement on November 12:

... At the same time, social deterioration was taking place. The passivity imposed on the government by the seizing of hostages brought about a vacuum in the action of public authority. People began to realize that the support shown for the FLQ manifesto by some movements like FRAP and the Central Council of the CSN in Montreal, plus a far less energetic condemnation of the FLQ's violent action, and the notices announcing meetings in the universities, gave a hint of some sympathy which could quite easily become active in the FLQ's favour. In these circumstances, even if there weren't so many active members of the FLQ, there was a serious possibility that some sympathizers would be swayed to activism or, under cover of support for the manifesto, would be drawn into uncontrolled movements or even that with all the muddle of true and false FLQ communiqués the temperature would be raised to the point where society might be seriously affected as far as its confidence in the government was concerned and that therefore general disorder would ensue.

It therefore became necessary for the government to assume its full responsibilities and to prevent the situation from getting worse, quite apart from the fact that the state of confusion which existed could not help to save the lives of Mr Cross or Mr Laporte. For, if you recall, as far as Mr Cross was concerned, after Saturday, October 10, no news was heard from the Liberation cell and it was only after the enforcement of the Emergency Measures and the death of Mr Laporte that proof of his still being alive was given.

Consequently if we just consider the escalation which came about because of the Chenier cell, which was obviously much less well organized – that is becoming quite obvious now – than the Liberation cell, the Chenier cell created a very ambiguous situation, giving the impression of some sort of strategy – even now I don't entirely exclude this – so that the state had no other choice than to react as radically as possible, for everything led us to believe in a planned and united effort on the part of FLQ members to stir up disorder to hysterical proportions and to introduce such a chaos as would prove explosive and upset the organization of the whole country.

Therefore the government had to take appropriate steps to deal with a situation which might prove dangerous to public order. The arrival of the armed forces earlier in the day of October 15 lessened the load borne by the police in the City of Montreal and the Quebec Police Department, by taking over the work of guards so they could carry on with their proper police work.

This measure, which was followed by the implementation of regulations governing public order on October 16 and the detention of several noisy FLQ sympathizers, caused the following results:

Firstly, dislocation of the plan, or somewhat improvized strategy if you like, covering propaganda, public demonstrations, and instructions aimed at the disorganization of society and the state.

Secondly, the fact that the terrorists were forced to cut themselves off and go underground.

Thirdly, a dampening, albeit temporary, of student ardour or that of other movements sympathetic with the manifesto, since the FLQ had been declared illegal.

Fourthly, the seizure of a considerable amount of firearms and dynamite.

Fifthly, the discovery of proof of acts of sedition and terrorism, as well as information concerning terrorist activity.

On Saturday evening, October 17, we learned of the murder of Pierre Laporte. Communiqué no 6 from the Chenier cell announced that the execution had been carried out by the Dieppe cell. Subsequently other communiqués announced the appearance on the scene of other FLQ cells ...

Prime Minister Bourassa's statement on October 16 that the government feared a fourth stage of assassination was regarded as a loophole in the official argument. Since Lucien Saulnier was often credited with the information, journalists and politicians checked back through the documents made public at the appearance of Mr Saulnier before a House committee in November 1969 during the CYC hearings and found in the *Stratégie révolutionnaire et rôle de l'avant-garde*, supposedly written by Pierre Vallières, a three-stage plan – the radicalization of social agitation, the establishment of local liberation committees, and finally armed confrontation. Finding no evidence, they regarded the fear of assassination as another Trudeau-Bourassa-Drapeau myth. They overlooked the open adoption of the tactics of urban guerilla warfare in numerous FLQ tracts including the *Stratégie révolutionnaire*. Moreover, there had been, as Ottawa and Quebec knew well, some FLQ discussions about assassinations. (They may perhaps have known more, for there were repeated journalistic references to documents in the hands of the government which mentioned kidnapping and assassination and even named some of the likely targets.) A writer in *Victoire* (June 24, 1969) an official organ of the FLQ, observed:

> I have been thinking about the assassinations mentioned in an FLQ communiqué. Although this plan does not seem altogether useless, I do not recommend it. Or, in any event, it should not be put into practice until a close analysis of all the consequences it might have has been made. We have seen what martyrs have been made out of the Kennedy brothers and Martin Luther. The martyr has this particularity, he attracts sympathy. We should not like to see a Trudeau, a Bertrand, or any other victim of an assassination. This would be a good turn to the cause which they are defending!

The accusation that Mr Trudeau had imposed the army and the War Measures Act on Quebec was as insistent as the charge that apprehended insurrection was a myth. Reputable journalists, professional and academic, were unhesitating in their statement of "fact," and left-wing magazines described the crisis with such categorical copy as "War Declared on Quebec" (*Canadian Dimension*, December) and "The Ploy against Quebec" and "The Santo Domingo of Pierre Elliott Trudeau" (*Last Post*, no 5), or a Parti pris title *Québec occupé*.

Once again the two governments repeatedly denied the charge. Why is it, Bourassa asked in the Assembly on November 12, "that every time we collaborate with the federal government, every time there is any sort of co-operation, this should necessarily be subordination?" At a November 5 press conference he revealed that he had called Trudeau the night Laporte was kidnapped:

La ligne dure

Le Devoir, Montreal, November 9, 1970

As I have already said, when Mr Laporte was abducted anything could have followed. At that time I considered it my responsibility to telephone the Prime Minister of Canada, who had jurisdiction over the army and the War Measures Act, and to tell him to take steps to make the army available if I needed it during the next few days or later, or maybe not at all, and similarly that he should be ready to adopt the War Measures Act if the situation called for it.

As a matter of fact, he explained to the *Gazette* (December 3):

I talked to him many times during the crisis. If I had said to Mr Trudeau Thursday: "No, it will be Friday, and I insist it will be Friday," he would have said it was Friday. I think this was clear. When I spoke to him on Saturday night, he said: "You don't ask for it now." I said: "No, not for now, but keep it available." That was the night they kidnapped Pierre Laporte ... So it was Quebec which had the power to decide, and we decided ...

Questioned on "Format 60" by Louis Martin, who expressed the view that it was scandalous that Ottawa not Quebec called the shots, Trudeau replied:

> But I don't think it's at all scandalous. On the contrary, this is what happened. Quebec played the predominant part. It was Quebec, the Quebec government, elected six months ago with a large majority of the seats, that asked for the army to come. Despite the fact that for several days the federal government was saying: maybe things shouldn't be done too quickly. It was the government of Quebec and of Montreal that asked us to enforce the extraordinary act, the War Measures Act. They had been asking us for it for some days. They didn't ask for it outright; they said: keep it in mind, we may have to use that act. And we in the federal government said to them: isn't there any other way to handle this? We were trying more to delay the War Measures Act. It was Quebec and Montreal who took the initiative to say: now's the time to act. I am not saying that we ourselves didn't think this should be done too, but the initiative did not come from us. The first people to ask me to invoke this act were the authorities in Quebec and Montreal, and I think that all things considered they were right. I am not trying to pass the buck. I think it is a mistake to say that it wasn't Quebec that took the initiative and that Ottawa tried every way it could to sway Quebec over to our way of thinking. That is all quite wrong.

Those who rejected the plausibility of an apprehended insurrection, whether defined as uncontrollable civil disorder or armed confrontation through more bombing, kidnappings, and assassinations, were usually unshakeable in their conviction that Trudeau had imposed his will on the government of Quebec. The association was necessary; the interpretation was clear. Ann Charney (*Canadian Forum*, January 1971), for example, saw throughout the crisis "an inclination on the part of the federal government to use the kidnapping as a way of confronting the real opposition in Quebec, that is, the wide spectrum of political, economic and social groups united through their belief in an independent Quebec." The *Canadian Dimension* staff agreed that the War Measures Act gave Mr Bourassa, with a divided cabinet and under the thumb of Trudeau, "a momentary reprieve"; Mayor Drapeau a chance to crush "serious opposition"; and Mr Trudeau the opportunity "to stamp out separatism, especially the Parti Québécois." *Last Post*, like Ann Charney, emphasized the widespread support for the FLQ manifesto, and the pressure for the release of the prisoners after the kidnapping of Laporte. "It is a matter of general agreement among the Ottawa press corps," wrote the editors, that it was the Holiday Inn statement of October 14, "that tripped the balance. Trudeau realized he was losing ground in Quebec, that a floodtide of opposition to Ottawa was rising. The Bourassa government was divided, but a new alliance of socialists and liberals and separatists and labor threatened to fill the vacuum." *Last Post* quoted Liberal MP Patrick Mahoney's statement at Calgary on October 20 that the Holiday Inn statement prompted the use of the War Measures Act because it tended "to give leadership in the direction of eroding the will to resist FLQ demands," and Anthony Westell (*Toronto Star*, October 17) wrote:

> Only a few weeks before, Lévesque's separatists had been extremists on the Quebec spectrum. With the emergence of terrorism as the new extreme, the perspective changed. Suddenly Lévesque was appearing with Montreal editor Claude Ryan, a nationalist, on a platform urging peace with the FLQ – a new, moderate centre, as it appeared to some.
>
> For Trudeau, the moment for decisive action to stop the drift in opinion was rapidly approaching.

To the *Last Post* all was clear: "the opinions of Québécois who did not support the FLQ but shared some of the views the FLQ and the left have been voicing for years were apparently not to be tolerated. Pierre Elliott Trudeau had to suspend democracy." It was in effect a coup d'état, a shift in political power to Ottawa which not only enabled Trudeau to crush nationalist and socialist opposition but also, said Jacques Parizeau, provided him with the opportunity to establish "the inevitable confrontation which had to come sooner or later between Ottawa and Quebec."

These same critics saw the provisional government plot as a planned attempt to smear the nationalist opposition. The "plot," whose foundation in fact seems to have been the October 11 alternative hypotheses and conversations of Claude Ryan which certainly revealed his fear of the breakdown of civil authority, was largely the creation of the press. It first appeared in the *Toronto Star* on October 26:

> Top-level sources indicated today that Prime Minister Pierre Trudeau's decision to invoke the War Measures Act was based on something more than fear of the Front de libération du Québec's plan for the "well-organized escalation of terror" to which Pierre Laporte referred in his agonized plea for freedom.
>
> According to these informants, the factor that finally drove the Trudeau government into action was that they became convinced a plan existed to replace the Quebec government of Premier Robert Bourassa. The Trudeau administration believed that a group of influential Quebeckers had set out to see whether they might supplant the legitimately elected provincial government with what they conceived of as an interim administration having enough moral authority to restore public order.

The story was universally believed to have been written by Peter Newman; and the top-level sources to have been Bryce Mackasey, among other cabinet ministers, politicians, and civil servants to whom Newman talked during a visit to the capital. Once Newman had broken the story other reporters soon professed to find their sources.

The next day Bourassa issued a press communiqué stating that "he had been informed of the likelihood of such a plan, but that the government had been in no way influenced in its decisions by such an unlikely possibility." In the Commons the Prime Minister replied to a question by David Lewis: "I would not deny that we were not aware of rumours which were circulating or of other types of information which may or may not be substantiated. I am just saying that we acted on the information which is known to the House ..." Claude Ryan at once assumed not only that the alleged plot involved him but that it was the continuation of an Ottawa plot to destroy nationalist opposition. As he wrote in *Le Devoir* (October 28):

> ... So a theory has been worked out in Ottawa of a plot aimed at removing Mr Bourassa from power and replacing him by a "provisional government" for the purpose of bringing Quebec under the rule of the FLQ. And everything has been done (cocktail parties ideally suited for the spreading of wild rumours, appeals to the left and the right from the régime's "errand boys," etc.) so as to give substance to this theory.
>
> But it was so outlandish that the more they tried to put it over the more ridiculous and stupid it seemed. I was going to say malicious, but I am not too certain about that. Mr Trudeau and his friends are after certain dissident elements: but I don't think they are capable of sinking so low. I would rather believe that they were carried away by panic.
>
> They must justify to English Canada a decision the gravity of which cannot be explained away by the facts presently known to the public. Since the explanations so far given are not enough in themselves to reassure some people, others have to be found.
>
> What could be more tempting in such a situation than to invent, on the basis of vague items of gossip taken out of their context, an explanation implying conspiracy involving such well-known citizens as Lévesque, Laberge, Pépin, Rouleau, Parizeau, Kirouac, Daoust, Ryan, etc.? The only disadvantage to this explanation is that it doesn't hold water and that it brings out into the open how much at a loss were the people who invented it and who, as one of their most respected intimates informs us, are "top-level sources" ...

The Prime Minister's reply to a question in the House that morning did little to enlighten the country – or conciliate the press: "I would be delighted if the journalists were to identify the 'top level sources' on which they always base their false reports, but I am surprised to see that it is a journalist who is asking other journalists to disclose their sources, and I am delighted about that." With the press spreading and building the provisional government story, Claude Ryan wrote the lengthy editorial of October 30 (see pp. 63–4). But the story continued to grow, and take strange forms. While Ryan was claiming that he was being smeared by Trudeau, Dominique Clift, using his own top-level sources, was writing that both Bourassa and Ryan were involved:

La Presse, Montreal, November 11, 1970

> Premier Robert Bourassa himself was at the very centre of the consultations which could have led to the formation of a government of national unity in Quebec, a move which was later misrepresented by Mayor Jean Drapeau and anonymous federal sources as an attempt to create a provisional government sympathetic to the cause of revolution.
>
> The reasoning in circles close to the premier was that such a government of national unity, taking in representatives from other political parties and other groups, would enhance the authority of the cabinet in facing revolutionary agitation and at the same time ensure its freedom of action against a preponderant federal influence (*Montreal Star*, November 2).

The new cabinet, wrote Clift, would have included Lévesque, Marcel Pépin, Louis Laberge, and possibly Ryan. "One of the intermediaries used for assessing the feasibility of such a move was Claude Ryan. However, it is not clear yet whether he was acting according to a definite mandate or had merely received a vague and general encouragement to explore a possibility which he himself had put to the premier." At his November 5 press conference Premier Bourassa admitted that he had spoken to Lévesque and Ryan, but vigorously denied that he discussed a union government. Whatever the real story – if there was a story at all –

the provisional government plot promised to become a permanent part of the history of the crisis.

More important, perhaps, it was an indicator of the immediate consequences of the crisis on Quebec and Canadian politics and society – the excessive and unqualified polarization of opinion. Despite their repudiation of the Front's methods, those who endorsed the manifesto seemed ambiguous and ambivalent. Despite their abhorrence of the murder and kidnapping, those who appealed for the release of the twenty-three "political prisoners" seemed somehow to be accepting the FLQ analysis and condoning terrorism for cause. Quebec was split between hawks – 75 per cent wrote Charles Taylor, no friend of the establishment – and the doves. But Solange Chaput-Rolland's report that in Montreal "if you belong to one of these factions, you will be wise to mix, receive, visit, discuss and have a drink with your own group of friends, otherwise your evenings or your meetings might be transferred into a battle ground" was equally true in other parts of Canada.

The effect of this polarization was more than social, and would last long after the crisis ended. It divided union leaders from their members, and led some to conclude that political non-intervention was essential. It led Michel Cartier to withdraw from FRAP until "such time as the present ambiguous attitude of the Permanent Council towards terrorism had been resolved" (unpublished letter, November 9). And it forced Paul Cliche to make a public statement denouncing "all terrorism and especially that practised by the FLQ." If it was not done immediately, he told the Permanent Council, FRAP will break up and will lose the character of a movement seeking to organize the mass of salaried workers politically" (unpublished letter to the council, November 12). But on a motion of Henri Bellemare on November 15 the council voted 15 to 5 for the resignation of Mr Cliche.

The polarization led some journalists to conclude that Mr Bourassa lost the support of the intellectuals and leaders of left-wing and nationalist opinion who previously would not move as far or as fast as Rene Lévesque. It led members of the left to believe that the democratic mobilization of the Québécois for massive social and economic reform had become impossible (a conclusion reinforced by the post-crisis history of FRAP). As Laurier LaPierre wrote to his friend Cy Gonick of *Dimension* (December 1970):

> After all this terrible war that has been decreed has little to do with the FLQ. It has much to do however with the unknown, of the inevitable confrontation between men who seek freedom and those who possess it and want to dish it

out only to their friends. IF WE ARE NOT TO HAVE A REVOLUTION IN OUR FREE, LEFT, NON-VIOLENT DEMOCRATIC WAY – MUST WE BE CO-OPTED INTO THE SYSTEM OR TURN TO VIOLENCE? THAT HAS BECOME – AT LEAST FOR ME – THE QUESTION.

If that had become the question, the FLQ had succeded beyond all measure.

More sober and reflective analysts attempted to gauge the effect of the crisis on the FLQ. Many English Canadians agreed with the *Winnipeg Free Press* (October 19) that the War Measures Act "spelled the death of the FLQ," but others uneasily noted that among the articulate minority and the young the heroes of the crisis in Quebec seemed to be, if not the kidnappers, the four horsemen – Lemieux, Chartrand, Vallières, and Gagnon. Charles Taylor (*Ottawa Citizen*, October 19) suggested that the "FLQ sympathisers will undergo a mutation. Some will break away, but the rest will have to change. They know now that they can kill or condone killing. At first there will be much fewer of them. Most sympathizers live on the illusion that nothing terrible would happen. They could perhaps have accepted the death of the hostages in the heat of a shoot-out with the police, but the cold-blooded brutal murder of Pierre Laporte will repel them. Those that remain, however, will be ready to condone anything."

University of Montreal sociologist Guy Rocher had no doubt that the FLQ had won, and its movement strengthened by the events of October. As he wrote in *Québec-Presse* (October 25):

... For the time being the government has won, but the real victor is the FLQ. Beyond even what the FLQ was hoping for. I am not very happy to to say this – I am stunned – but the analysis made by the Félquistes is being proved right. They stirred up fear, panic, disorganization of government administration; they sowed discord, weakened provincial government, and the list could go on. And it is a favourable list according to the FLQ's logic.

It will take a long time to recoup. It will take months and months to shake off the rottenness caused by the FLQ operation. Yet again, and it is painful for me to say, I believe that the FLQ has gained more than is generally believed.

I do not share the analytical methods or ideology of the FLQ, but it has proved an important sociological truth: terror can be phenomenally and devastatingly efficient. It is such a powerful type of action that we can't use it. Terrorism should be banished like the atomic bomb! Terrorism has a lot in common with the atomic bomb: the fallout is very widespread. This is a useful comparison.

The government has entered into revolutionary warfare, and that is a serious mistake. Even a moral mistake. One day, sooner or later, we will realize that, instead of condemning revolutionary war it walked straight into it. It played the same game and gave extra power to the FLQ's action. The FLQ wanted to create a state of war and the government was completely taken in.

More important was the effect of the crisis on the democratic separatist movement. On that the *Winnipeg Free Press* (October 19) had no doubts: "The murder of Mr. Laporte should, if there is any justice, sound the death knell of the separatist movement in Quebec. If it does, his death, tragic as it has been, will not have been in vain." Quite clearly the *Free Press* was incapable of distinguishing between Péquistes and Félquistes, or of accepting any middle ground between hawks and doves. Nevertheless, the Parti québécois may have suffered because of the crisis.

Gilles Lalande, a Montreal political scientist, declared that "La vague séparatiste ... vient de mourir" because the FLQ, FRAP, and others had so clearly linked ultra-radicalism with ultra-nationalism. In his interview with Louis Martin on "Format 60," Prime Minister Trudeau observed that "some separatist leaders and many others have supported, you might say, the objectives of the FLQ" and "at least one FLQ aim: a government agreement to free prisoners." In reply to Martin's question "That makes them accomplices, does it not?" the Prime Minister said: "Not at all ... I find – and I am answering your question – perhaps they identified themselves in the public mind not with the use of violence but with the demands of those who were using it." Mr Trudeau's discretion was not shared by Mr Choquette during the November 13 debate in the Assembly. Vigorously attacking the Parti québécois, he asked: "But in fact might these preachers of non-violence be hawks disguised under the convenient feathers of doves? Behind these all to easy escapist solutions of the Parti québécois and its leader in particular, might there not exist a calculated political move aimed at undermining present democratic institutions? This seems quite obvious to me."

Yet if some were driven from separatism by the ambiguity of its leaders or the rhetoric of Choquette, others may have been driven closer by the seeming futility of the decade-old struggle to improve conditions in the province. On several occasions Claude Ryan said that the crisis forced a basic re-examination of Quebec society and its relations with Ottawa. In a November 9 editorial he denied that he had moved over to René Lévesque, but wrote that two basic questions had to be answered:

1 Might not the types of political and social structures under which we live be responsible, to an extent yet to be determined, for the continual crises which we have witnessed?
2 Will these same structures be capable, in the case of fresh crises threatening on the horizon, of bringing about peace, liberty, and prosperity – without which political life is hardly worth living – for our society?

Although Mr Ryan promised to keep his readers informed as he moved along the road, it appeared to many that he had already reached his destination. It may be that many others, hoping above all to find peace in a troubled Quebec, had also. And in English Canada there were some nationalists of the left, like Abraham Rotstein, who seemed to see the October crisis as the prelude to an armed confrontation if Quebec reached separatism by democratic means. "We must now travel in tandem," he wrote in the *Canadian Forum* (January 1971) "to create in English Canada active legal, political and institutional channels that support and foster Quebec's legitimate aspirations. It is our only hope of mitigating the impact of the collision which looms ahead."

If the crisis reminded Canadians of the fragility of civil liberties when law and order or the foundations of the state seem threatened, it also aroused a latent right-wing sentiment in the country. The overwhelming approval of the War Measures Act stunned civil libertarians, particularly in English Canada. Some journalists saw the government's attempts to impose moderation on the media, as well as the discussions of press censorship in the cabinet, not as an attempt to cool a crisis continually heated by the press but as a pretext to create a subservient press. The media did not set a high standard. "The mania," said *Last Post,* became "the message ..." James Cross watched his own death announced on television, and could have read it in the papers. No rumour was too outrageous, no speculation too foolish, to be broadcast and printed. Yet views still differed: If the *Last Post* could charge the media with capitulation to the establishment, Jean Pellerin could write that "we had the feeling that Radio-Canada and some private radio stations had become the anarchists tribunals. The latter did in all events use the state radio as a platform for spreading hate and verbal violence" (*La Presse,* October 26).

In Ottawa there were demands for the re-establishment of capital punishment, and in Quebec on November 13 Mr Choquette promised legislation in 1971 which could include compulsory identification cards, provincial emergency powers, provisions for the establishment of press censorship, and the extension of police powers to fight organized crime. During the debate a Liberal backbencher called for the drafting of young radicals, a view that in principle could be found across the country. Certainly the use of young radicals as social animators, paid by CYC or welfare funds, was more closely examined, at least by the establishment. As Mr Saulnier's evidence the previous November had revealed, and the crisis underlined, social animation often had been replaced by an ideology which demanded the tactics of muscular and sometimes violent confrontation.

The educational system, already the dismay of many anxious parents, came under closer scrutiny. Jean Pellerin (*La Presse,* October 26) suggested that "the educator's task is to teach, and not to be an organ of political propaganda or social activism." The majority of teachers did just that, he argued, but "a minority is making a greater effort to arouse the young people and spends most of its time organizing so-called spontaneous demonstrations. This minority is cheating, and the government must make it mend its ways. The taxpayer is not paying heavy school taxes so that the first visionary to come along can consider it his right to indoctrinate his offspring." Soon afterward the Quebec government appointed an educational ombudsman who, among other duties, would study parental complaints about classroom indoctrination.

At the universities, Pellerin continued, "the atmosphere is not entirely healthy ... The police have just seized an edition of the *Quartier Latin* which was being prepared. This edition was to contain an article about politicians who should be annihilated. Prime Ministers Trudeau and Bourassa came at the head of the list. They were intending to publish photos of them filled with bullet holes". Appearing on "60 Minutes" (CBS, December 8) Mr Trudeau told interviewer Mike Wallace that

> ... in 1961 a policy was affirmed and then reaffirmed I believe in '63 or '64 that there would be no police surveillance on university campuses and so on in the name of freedom of thought and the freedom of teaching and so on. And it was at this time a good decision. But it is apparent that if the revolutions and the revolts are going to begin on campuses – and it is apparent that if the instigators of violent dissent are going to find their natural milieu there, there can be no more exception for the intellectual part of the community in the name of academic freedom, than there can be for you and me in the name of any other freedom.

Whatever the future of the FLQ, the October crisis was a turning point in Canadian history. Superficially it forced a re-examination of Quebec nationalism, and the relations between Quebec and the rest of Canada. Far more important, however, it forced a re-examination of fundamental attitudes, beliefs, and values. The nationalism of the FLQ might be limited and contained; its radicalism brought Canada fully into the last half of the century, for it challenged less the existence of the nation-state than the nature of the society within it.